PUTTING HAND TO THE PLOUGH

A MEMOIR

DENIS O'CALLAGHAN

Published 2007 by
Veritas Publications
7/8 Lower Abbey Street
Dublin 1
Ireland
Email publications@veritas.ie
Website www.veritas.ie

ISBN 978 1 84730 026 3

Copyright © Denis O'Callaghan, 2007

A catalogue record for this book is available from the British Library.

Designed by Colette Dower
Printed in the Republic of Ireland by Betaprint, Dublin

Veritas books are printed on paper made from the wood pulp of managed
forests. For every tree felled, at least one tree is planted, thereby renewing
natural resources.

CONTENTS

FOREWORD

Arrival at one's seventy-fifth birthday gives one an opportunity to draw breath while looking back over the journey to date. That journey for me has run through three phases – twenty-five years to priesthood for the Diocese of Cloyne, twenty-five years teaching moral theology in Maynooth, twenty-five years ministering as parish priest in Mallow. In hindsight that tripartite life seems to me all of a piece, one phase leading into the next. The first section on growing up at home in Meelin may seem out of kilter but it was the most formative time of my life. Nature and nurture combined there to make me what I am, for good or ill, as man and priest. The rest after that was more or less natural progression in response to circumstances and challenges. The call to priesthood was never far away.

What I have composed is best described as a memoir. It reflects personal impressions as I have passed various milestones in life. When potholers explore a cave they leave a marking line along the way. It is on the more relaxed return journey that major features hold attention and register significance. I find that memory for me operates by association of ideas around recall of experiences. That leads to a chain of thought which suits the style of a memoir. Researching and analysing theological concepts, which was second nature to me when in Maynooth, demands a different approach. One is then writing for a more identifiable professional audience who require something beyond setting out personal experiences and impressions. I will still deal with theological concepts here but in a more pastoral context which reflects personal assessments rather than focuses on abstract analyses. To employ that overused cliché, I may have talked the talk in Maynooth but I have walked the walk in Mallow.

In a memoir one aims to be honest but one also wishes to be sensitive to personal feelings. Fr Denis Meehan, Professor of Latin in Maynooth, wrote a pleasant informative book on the historical associations of the College. It was titled *I Remember Maynooth*. A later volume, *Maynooth Again Remembered*, was far more astringent, particularly in its assessment of deceased colleagues. Fr John McMackin, Professor of English and master of the rapier in exchanges at table, commented that this book added a new horror to the fear of dying.

Cardinal John Carmel Heenan employed as title for his life story *Not the Whole Truth*. I am not sure what he intended by this. I intend to be as fair as I can. A canonist friend has reminded me of a legal witticism to the effect that to tell the truth is difficult, to tell the whole truth is impossible but to tell the truth and nothing but the truth is disastrous! If I need to be economical with the truth where third parties are concerned it will not affect the substance. Blandness is not in my nature. There is no sense in plying sleeping dogs with tranquillisers where some issue requires a wake-up call.

In that context I will target what I think should be a major concern for the Catholic Church here, the concern about clericalism, which is more prevalent among the secular clergy. The religious are more committed to collaborative ministry. There is a definite gender factor also at work. The National Council of Priests of Ireland has organised a series of workshops throughout the country on the theme *Priestly Morale and Collaboration between Clergy and Laity*. This is certainly the way forward. We pride ourselves on our pastoral expertise, on not being 'sacristy priests'. Yet we seem to lack vision for the way ahead with a seriously depleted number of priests in the ranks. Our prevailing clerical mindset may have confined us in a straitjacket when new thinking and fresh planning is essential if the Gospel is to have its effect on the Ireland of today and tomorrow.

We speak of how our Church has been affected on so many fronts by the blight of clerical sex abuse. One area in which we have been seriously affected is the manner in which energy has been sapped. It has left us too long in defensive mode with that crisis call of 'all hands to the pumps'. We do indeed have critics who regard the Catholic Church as dead in the water. We need to build confidence by a radical refit and so get underway on the course of pastoral ministry into the future. That future promises further white water for a society which has dragged its anchors. The message of the Gospel inspired by the Holy Spirit will be more relevant than ever in that fractured world.

Whatever time the Lord grants me I hope and pray to be part of that future. I chose as title for the memoir *Putting Hand to the Plough*. It comes from that challenge of Jesus: 'No one putting hand to the plough and looking back is fit for the Kingdom of God' (Luke 9:62). If anyone needs faith in Christ confirmed one cannot do better than take St Paul's courage and vision to heart. His words ring as bright and true today as they did two thousand years ago. How one would like to share the confidence of St Paul in his letter to Timothy, his close associate in the Ministry, to the effect that having fought the good fight, having finished the race and having kept the faith he now looks forward to an eternal reward (2 Tim 4:6-8).

CHAPTER 1

GROWING UP IN MEELIN

Meelin is a village tucked into that corner of the map where the county of Cork meets Kerry and Limerick. It was not just the place where I first saw the light on 4 March 1931. It became my home in every sense – physically, emotionally and spiritually. It was close enough to the heartland of Sliabh Luachra to benefit from that rich culture of story and song. The village was ideally situated to take full advantage of the landscape. The vista to the south stretched away to the mountain range beyond Millstreet. This provided us with the short-term weather forecast, 'Ceo ar Muisire 's Clárach lom an chómartha soinnine is fearr ar domhann' (Muisire in fog with Clarach clear, what better promise that sun is near). To the north we were sheltered by high ground which gave the village its name. *Maoileann* from the Irish *maol* describes a flat-topped hill and is found in many place names. It does not sound very romantic but it was a welcome physical feature in our landscape. Local lore added to the romance by creating the legend that Moylan's Rock on the brow of the hill was favoured by the presence of a *bean sí* for whom the village was named.

My Christian names 'Denis Francis' were not matters of choice. They were *given* names, in the literal sense of that word. The Denis was the patronymic which interchanged with John in sequence through the eldest sons from generation to generation in the O'Callaghan family. This handing on of names was common practice in families at that time. By the

8

way, that practice has greatly assisted those who now engage in the task of tracing family roots.

The 'Francis' was the second of the given names inherited by me from my grandfather. He had been baptised simply Denis. The addition of Francis was a mystery to me until I discovered a little diary in which he had made some entries during his sojourn in Australia as a young man. There he notes that in Sydney on 17 July 1892 he had been initiated into the Third Order of St Francis by a Capuchin priest. My grandfather directed as follows: 'I wish to have this name included whilst in this world and also after my death in any inscription where my name is mentioned.' It is so recorded on his gravestone in Clonfert cemetery.

This surely explains his devotion to the Capuchin Friars right through his life. For his marriage in 1903 to Mary Ellen Roche, a national teacher in Meelin, they went to Cork. The priest who blessed the marriage there was a Capuchin Father from Holy Trinity Church in that city. My mother told me that my grandfather had hoped that in time I would join the Capuchin Franciscans. There were still many years to go before that option arose for me.

My mother, Mary Sheehy, a native of Freemount, was a national school teacher in Meelin. She was a woman of strong mind and will and would take the side of anyone whom she knew to have been unfairly treated. It was no mean feat at the time to challenge a parish priest who had hoped to move out of the parish a young girl, a former school pupil, who had become pregnant. He had wished to distance the scandal from his area of responsibility while the bishop was on visitation. In her firm stand she showed something of the character of Hannah Sheehy-Skeffington, to whom she was related on her father's side. As an early campaigner for women's rights that lady is remembered in a fine bronze sculpture in Kanturk's riverside park. My mother breast-fed me for six months. This must have been quite unusual at the time. I never heard from her the reason for it. It must have been difficult for her – and for me! – as the feeds would have been separated by the six hours or so of the school day. By all accounts I was a placid child: so I was told by Nurse Burke from Newmarket, the midwife who delivered me at home in Meelin, and who was held in high regard by the family. My mother once asked me my earliest memory of herself. It was a memory of her putting up patterned paper on a kitchen press. I would have been in the pram, all of six months waving my hands, she recalled, as the paper crinkled. Early evidence of a do-it-yourselfer!

My father, John O'Callaghan, Jack Denny O as he was known, as an only son inherited the farm in Meelin. He was a great man for reading, like his father before him. In those days, as the saying went, one read the old *Freeman's Journal* and later *The Cork Weekly Examiner* from stem to stern. There are also some well-thumbed books at home, now over a century old. One book which has not survived was a collection of heroic tales from ancient times. The stories of the doings of Fionn and the Fianna were writ larger than either life or legend warranted. The story that made a lasting impression on me was that of the Spartan King Leonidas who, with three hundred men, held the pass at Thermopylae against a huge invading Persian army. I got my grandfather to read it to me again and again. The sense of *genius loci* brought it all back to me when I stood in that Pass of Thermopylae thirty years later and read the Greek inscription composed after the battle in 480 BC: 'Go tell the Spartans you who pass by that here obedient to their laws we lie.'

Education featured high in Meelin even before the national school was established in the village in July 1856. Before that there was a range of hedge schools at various sites in the parish. John Browne, a hedge school master in Knockeen, west of Meelin, became the first principal. He was one of many hedge school teachers who were later appointed to national schools. This information was given in a letter to me by Jeremiah Browne, retired national teacher in Meelin. The recall in that letter is amazing in view of the fact that he had just celebrated his hundredth birthday! There is a tradition in my family that a granduncle John O'Callaghan attended a hedge school in Barleyhill where the Black Master, Edmond Hannon, taught. That teacher must have had a major focus on mathematics as there is a certificate from the London Science and Art Department of the Privy Council on Education to the effect that in the examination held on 10 May 1886 John O'Callaghan obtained a First Class Honours in the first stage of Mathematics. At that time he was an officer of the excise branch of the Inland Revenue to which he had been appointed on 17 March 1881.

On the margins and back of that 1881 parchment there are listed the various places where he served. The writing is now almost indecipherable. There is a story in the family that he was killed in a fall from a horse following a wager with a friend. The horse had been bought at a premium in sovereigns in the horse fair at Cahirmee where at the time there was stiff competition with buyers for cavalry mounts in European armies.

Now to get back to Meelin as I knew it. In today's world where technology and mobility rule the lives of our young people they would be in disbelief at how full our lives were then. There were seven of us in the family: five girls and two boys. Another boy, John, was still an infant when he contracted pneumonia. Before the days of sulpha drugs this was all too often a death sentence. I cannot recall much illness in our home, thank God. At the age of four I suffered a perforated appendix and was rushed for emergency surgery to Cork Bons Secours hospital. I spent quite a while there. I did not miss home that much because I made friends with a girl of the same age. Mary Wallace's parents visited the hospital frequently and they took me under their wing as well. I also got to know an intern, Dr Raymond Cross. The attraction there was his little red sports car! Thirty years later we met up again when I called to his consulting rooms in Dublin's Fitzwilliam Square for his direction on some issue of medical ethics which I was researching. He became a frequent guest at table in Maynooth. He was an outstanding entertainer, even through his final illness. May God reward him for his quiet generosity when patients could not afford a fee. Indeed, one mother was so delighted with the care and attention that she christened her child Raymond!

With many school companions in Meelin, boredom was never a factor in our early experience. Wordsworth noted that 'Bliss it was in that dawn to be alive. To be young was very heaven.' Oscar Wilde – or was it George Bernard Shaw? – may have felt that youth was too precious to be wasted on the young but it surely was not wasted on us! It has been said that schooldays are the happiest days of our lives. I doubt that this applied to the actual hours spent at desks in school. Still, the confinement gave fresh zest to the eventual freedom. We enjoyed that freedom, healthy and carefree in every sense of that word. For speed and agility the hare had nothing on us. 'Mar chos an ghiorrai do bhí mo chos, mar iarann gach alt 's féith. Bhí an solus rómhann tháll's a bhus 'san gleann 'nar tógadh mé.'

I suppose our young days in Meelin were typical of rural life in Cork at the time. Field sports centred pretty exclusively on hurling. Local farmers raised no objections to having their fields used for the rough and tumble of sport. It was an easy-going climate of give-and-take in the community. If you ran into a hazard in school or wherever, you took the blame yourself for any consequences, broken bones or whatever. There was no question of invoking liability under any health and safety rules or duty of care. We took in our stride whatever came. There was no one to blame but ourselves for our daredevil carelessness.

We must not forget the handball alley at the top of the village. This was a single high wall built from cut limestone. I assume that the building stood to the credit of the voluntary work of a group of local stonecutters. It served its purpose quite well even though the rough pebbled floor would severely punish a stumble. The alley also provided a meeting place for pitch-and-toss groups. Of a summer evening the competition would be hot and heavy. The skill of some players in landing their pennies right under the jack would leave modern snooker experts open-mouthed. The stakes might be pennies but honour was riding on every score.

Never a dull moment. Cowboys and Indians fought pitched battles in our grove and along the banks of the stream below the village. Yellow irises or *feilistrums* (in the Irish) served as casting spears when attacks were pushed home on some fortified Indian redoubt. On looking back on those times I can identify with Shakespeare's verse in *As You Like It*:

> And this our life exempt from public haunt,
> Finds tongues in trees, books in the running
> brooks, sermons in stones and good in everything.

There was that stream to be dammed to run water wheels to power contraptions linking up a series of thread reels with elastic bands serving as belts. The pool above the dam provided space for sailing homemade craft moulded from tins, some powered with recycled clock mechanisms. Lateral thinking was the order of the day. One did not then need the exploratory processes of a Transition Year programme to discover the potential of multiple intelligences.

Leisure activities were not laid on for us. We made our own sport. All that was needed was imagination to identify the possibilities in our surroundings. Improvisation was the name of the game. There was no such thing as pocket money! It was not today's money economy. Necessity was the mother of invention. That later has stood our generation well in the do-it-yourself stakes. An old Irish proverb has it that improvisation is a proof of wit: 'Is cuma le muc fear gan seift.' If we had a problem that called for a solution beyond our capabilities our grandad Denny O would be consulted. He was a mine of useful information and always ready to fund with a shilling or two if the case called for serious subsidy.

One of the best presents that came our way was a Spanish ass and cart left to us by our granduncle. Bill Roche had lived on the outside farm in Clashroe. Anyone who thinks an ass stupid never made the acquaintance of our animal. Once a rider got on his back, the ass would go straight for the nearest hedge. One then had the option of vacating one's seat ignominiously or being bushed in the thorns. An enterprising school friend planned to get the ass to jump over a pole. The ass had other ideas, opting to go under it instead. These circus acts were by the way. The ass really came into his own on fine Saturdays when excursions further afield would be planned. Priory Wood was a favoured destination as we packed into the cart heads and tails. Even as children we knew from school that Priory was once the home of John Philpot Curran, a great man of law, father of Sarah Curran whose grave was in the Church of Ireland cemetery at Newmarket. We also knew that the poem of Thomas Moore, 'She is far from the land where her young hero sleeps', referred to the man she would have married, the patriot Robert Emmet, executed in Dublin city. Her memory is well recalled in the beautiful bronze sculpture at the eastern entrance to Newmarket.

However, our outings did not focus on historical research. Priory Wood was just magic to young hearts and minds. Early in the year there would be drifts of bluebells; birds would be nesting; red squirrels would flash from tree to tree. Then in autumn there were hazelnuts and conkers by the bagful. The core of the day was the picnic. Bottles of milk with good solid bacon sandwiches and, if we were really lucky, thick slices of porter cake.

On a farm, life is not all play. There was work to be done and we would all pitch in, particularly in the summer, to save the hay and get the harvest home. It was no great imposition because we enjoyed the companionship and the sense of achievement. I have happy memories of mowing the hay. My father and I would take turns on the mowing machine while the other sharpened the sickles. He had taught me the skills of putting up a good edge and preserving the temper on the steel blade from exposure to the sun. I can still smell the aroma of newly mown hay, see the larks in song as they climbed the evening air, and hear the grasshopper strumming in the dry grass.

My father had a way with horses and would know when enough was enough. I can still see how he would read the onset of tiredness and his words would have been welcomed: 'That's it Bob; well done Peg.' Those horses would nuzzle him in gratitude for the kind thought. When tractors came into use he mourned for the old days. Where the tractor was just noise, the horse had been company.

We lived life at first hand and survived to tell the tale. I wonder what memories today's young people will salt away from hours spent with PlayStations? Nothing as vibrant as ours I feel. The memories have not dimmed over the years. I can still scent the aroma of the turf fire in the bog as the blue smoke curled up with its promise of food for us hungry youngsters. Tea in the bog had a special quality never to be equalled. A shovel brightened from work would serve well as frying pan for whatever in the line of primitive mixed grill was available. I recall one hungry day when marauding crows had cleaned out the cache of food which had been stashed in the shade of a turf bank. At this distance sentiment takes over and exorcises the recall of the back-breaking work of footing turf where every turn of the sod released a cloud of midges. How we envied those who wreathed their heads with pungent tobacco smoke. In the days before Deet we rubbed our faces with the pressed leaves of bog juniper and myrtle.

– COUNTRY LIFE –

It was a simple, healthy world. Our expectations were readily satisfied and so in our day-to-day lives we were quite happy. Advertising had not yet come to ratchet up those expectations to the must-have level of today's youth. Brand rivalry and peer pressure had not yet controlled the high ground of what gives meaning to life. For us, simple presents and small outings made big differences. The result was that any excitement or celebration outside the ordinary course of day-to-day life was something special.

Christmas was the highlight of the year, the holidays to which we counted down the days. There were the preparations which gave this feast its particular aura. There were the presents which preserved the make-believe of Santa Claus in spite of our private misgivings. There was the general air of good humour as greetings of Happy Christmas were exchanged. It certainly was a red-letter day in our annual calendar. Indeed it cast its spell over quite a spread of days until Little Christmas brought closure.

My memories focus on the search for red-berry holly, on the anxious wait for Santa Claus, on the gargantuan meal on Christmas Day. It was difficult for us to keep the overall religious factor in mind because of this carnival of the senses. I do recall that spiritual note being brought into focus on Christmas Eve at the lighting of the large white candle. My father would have us on our knees to pray for long-dead members of the family. This would surely have been a sombre interlude for our parents as they thought of Christmases long ago. It certainly did not dampen the feel-good factor of the current Christmas for us.

We did not have Midnight Mass in Meelin. The three Christmas Masses, which liturgically are to be said at midnight, at dawn and in daytime, were all celebrated in sequence on Christmas morning. The church would be extra packed with so many people returned home for the feast. There would be warm greetings as long-absent neighbours recognised and greeted one another.

Today we find it hard to imagine a world without telephones and motor cars. The fact was that in those times you really had to meet people face-to-face in order to make contact. This gave Christmas an added dimension and quality of life. We would tackle up the horse and trap and strike off to visit the relations. They in turn would come to visit us. In a farming community without cows to milk these were days of leisure. The adults would exchange news of the family among themselves. We youngsters would get to know our cousins and maybe play together whatever games had come the way as Christmas presents.

In our day, horses and bicycles were not for sport and exercise. They served a basic need for locomotion, for getting from one place to another. Like many of our neighbours we would have one horse geared for the road. Of course, roads in general then were surfaced with rough stone. The main roads might have been coated with tar and chip. For these, the horse would be shod with special studs to maintain a grip. One would take special pride in a half-blood animal spinning along in well turned out equipage. Horses of this quality would be saddled up for funerals and the group of riders were given the name 'Meelin Cavalry'.

The bicycles of that time were solid and made to last. There were none of the refinements of today's machines. They were basic. They needed to be basic to withstand the worst that the pot-holed roads put in their way. They were simple in construction. This presented us with a temptation which we indulged one Christmas as the men back from service with farmers returned to base camp in Meelin. The bikes were parked outside Quinlan's bar. With some spanners we interchanged saddles and handlebars on a few and awaited results as the revellers emerged. Imagine that for a feature on TV's *Candid Camera* of a later age! By today's standards it would certainly pass as harmless sport. Vandalism and mindless destruction was not in our purview. The only 'gangs' were tricksters such as those known as the Buckaroos. They might smoke out a card-playing group by placing a wet bag on a cottage chimney or paint red the horns of a white cow on the eve of a fair. Boys would be boys.

From my earliest days I loved everything about the countryside. Here, I was blessed in my parents. My father, a quiet observer of his surroundings on the farm, had spent a year in Pallaskenry Agricultural Institute. He could identify the various grasses on sight: ryegrass, fescue, cocksfoot, Yorkshire fog or whatever. Similarly the wildflowers, celandine, primrose, cowslip, bluebell, violet, anemone and whatever the turn of the seasons brought. He crusaded against noxious weeds, the dock, the thistle and the ragwort or *buachalán buí*. He would turn in his grave at the thought of today's infestation by ragwort. As a man who knew the countryside at a time when ragwort was controlled, he would shake his head in disbelief at the cranks on a campaign today to save the ragwort as fodder for the caterpillars of the cinnabar moth! My mother was a teacher in Meelin National School. Nature study would have been part of her programme in the Training College at Limerick. She still had the books. I read them from cover to cover and would then check the information on the ground. Eventually I had learned the names of all the common wildflowers in both English and Irish. In many cases the names were descriptive and so were readily remembered. My mother had a great feel for these imaginative names. The late John McGahern ends his *Memoir* addressed to his mother with whom he shared a love of nature: 'I want no shadow to fall on her joy and deep trust in God. She will face no false reproaches. As we retrace our steps, I will pick for her the wild orchid and the windflower.' I am happy to say Amen to that.

Years later when I came to study Latin and Greek I was surprised at how many of those technical botanical titles aptly described the plants themselves. Take the geranium, known as the crane bill from the shape of its seed pod. The name derives from the Greek term for crane, *geraunos*. Those Greek roots for plant names have a particular interest for me. If my mother had not been up to speed on them I would not be here! The strange ways of Providence! When she applied for the vacant post in Meelin National School she was interviewed by

Fr Timothy Crowley, a man who has left his mark in history as a fine Greek scholar. At interview, knowing that in the teacher training college she would then have studied Greek and Latin language roots, one of the questions which he asked her was to derive the term chrysanthemum, name of the now familiar potmum. On her reply that it was derived from the Greek words for *chruseus* (golden) and *anthos* (flower) he expressed himself satisfied that she was capable of teaching the children of Meelin and thereupon affirmed her appointment to the post. No formal assessment procedures in those days!

It was not just books that were sources of country lore. Many of the neighbours were close observers of nature. Across the road from our home we had a gentle neighbour, Mike Carthy. Like Seadhna in an tAthar Peadar O'Laoghaire's book, he had a little thatched house, 'tig beag ar thaobh na foithne'. I recall how he would point out on frosty nights the wrens and tits crowding into holes under the thatched eave.

Then Ben the Broc. I never knew his surname but learned recently that it was Quinlan. I assume that he got his nickname from the badger. Like his namesake he was out more by night than by day. He was a dab hand at crafting sally cribs to catch blackbirds in the haggard. He made birdlime from the sap of holly bark fermented in the ground and set on twigs near seeding thistles to capture goldfinches. He did not speak much generally but was never caught for an explanation of some natural phenomenon – except once. On my way of an early summer morning to bring the cows in for milking I noticed a drag mark on the dewy grass. Curious, I followed the trail to a depression in midfield. There were the corpses of four feral cats, each with the flattened grass track of its delivery from different points of the compass. Ben the Broc thought it might be the work of foxes which are certainly known to kill cats. But four in that location! It left Ben shaking his head.

My mother had an aunt in Feohanagh near Newcastle West. Ellen Sheehy's home was a long thatched farmhouse. She was a widow of many years. We as a family were always welcome.

We returned that welcome in later years when she came to live beside us in Meelin. If Meelin was off the beaten track Feohanagh was also a backwater. The people seemed to us quaint and easygoing. Years later Patrick McNabb wrote a thesis for his Ph.D. in UCC on the social attitudes of West Limerick. It was true to life in every detail as I recalled it. One saying which he recounts gives the flavour. As he concluded his set questionnaire he addressed a query about neighbourliness to a farmer who shared a yard with those next door. The farmer hooked his thumbs behind his gallowses and commented: 'You know, sir, we are that close that if one of us took a dose of Epsom Salts 'twould work on the pair of us.'

Auntie Sheehy was a colourful character. She prided herself on winning the gold medal for butter tasting which would have qualified her for that role in the Cork Butter Market. I do not think that she ever left home except perhaps to spend some time at work in the neighbouring creamery at Drumcollogher, which was Ireland's first co-operative venture. She had a wealth of anecdotes with which she regaled us at night around the fire as the crickets strummed. It was there I first heard of bees' wine. This was a sugar mixture to which a special yeast was added to cause fermentation. The result was a potent alcoholic brew. It got its name from the floating nodules of yeast which resembled honeybees. As the yeast grew to fill the container one needed to dispose of most of it so as to give space to restart the process. She said that on one occasion they came home from Mass to find the ducks flapping around the yard in an advanced state of intoxication. Later I wondered whether she had made up the story when I read Jimín Mháire Thaigh's similar account of the drunken gander in one of our Irish books. She also told us about a semi-dormant cat which had taken to sleeping in a barn on a nest of eggs where a hen had been laying out. In time he hatched out the eggs and the chickens took to him and followed him around as their mother. She claimed that *The Limerick Leader* had carried the story. It seemed a bit far-fetched even to us, credulous as we were.

What seemed closer to the truth was the account of a bitch which had been deprived of her pups. She then adopted a pair of piglets which the mother sow was unable to suckle.

You can imagine the range of pisheogs and ghost stories that kept our ears and eyes wide open around that fire at night. One particular story from the spirit world had strong evidence on its side as I discovered later from my mother who had it at first hand. She reported what she and her family had experienced on the way to Mass in Freemount. One of the girls had got out to open a gate on a right-of-way which passed through a neighbouring farmyard. There she began to speak to those neighbours as one might do on their way to Mass. The father froze with the reins in his hands because he knew that those two old people had died in the 'flu epidemic which had swept the country after the end of the war in 1918. Afterwards he went to the priest to arrange a Mass for the repose of their souls. There it is as I heard it.

They say that memory for smells is longest lasting of all. Whenever I get a strong whiff of wood smoke I recall Feohanagh. Turf was not available as fuel. This is what is generally used to keep the heat on the bastible cover for baking bread. The substitute was dried cow patties, *borran* in Irish. Then the aroma of her bread baked from brown flour with a shake of yellow meal! The local name for the bread sounded like 'yellow wasther'. I never derived its source. It did not feature in any dictionary.

One can see why it would have been difficult to better that for a summer holiday. A close runner-up was the time we would spend in Ballybunnion where my mother would take a house or 'lodge' for the duration. Forty miles was then seen as a long journey and Mark Brosnan would wonder whether the old Ford V-8 hackney with dodgy tyres would get the distance during the war years. However, it always did. Once there, we hit the ground running. Sand and sea set the course for action. There would be gathering of periwinkles on the Black Rocks at low tide, excursions to the mouth of the Cashen estuary or to the strand at Doon, exploration of the caves and visiting the Seven Sisters cavern. This last was high risk and off-bounds without adult presence. Unfortunately, time passed all too quickly and we said a sad good-bye to the friends we had made, particularly to a numerous family of Stacks from Duagh.

They were innocent times. Horseplay rather than romance carried the day. That romance awaited until I spent a month in the Gaeltacht of Beal-átha-an-Ghaorthaidh just before I signed on to St Colman's College in Fermoy. I was shy to make an approach until shortly before I left and then only at the urging of the *bean-a tí*, who saw that I was smitten. The Latin tag describes the changing times: *O Tempora, O Mores.*

– ANGLER'S PARADISE –

One of the happiest memories of my youth goes back to days on the banks of Dallow, Allow and Feale. I still recall the first trout I caught on a homemade hazel rod in the pool below Ballinatona bridge on the Dallow. The river was in full flood and that foolish unsuspecting trout swallowed the worm in the murky water. I was all of eight years. Was I proud? Was I what? And of course I was hooked for life. I thank the local anglers for building on my addiction. They were so supportive of my juvenile efforts. The bane of my life was the retired bank clerk Rory Sheehan. He patrolled the river as his personal stamping ground and saw us youngsters as intruders trespassing on his territory.

The Meelin angling fraternity were special. They must have been a patient lot to put up with my pestering them about the strange secret ways of fish and the tried and tested methods for catching them. It was Den Vaughan who fitted out my first fishing rod. It was during the 1939–1945 war that I cut the hazel rod on the way to Shanahan's Mill with my mother to have wheat ground into flour to add to the ration. Den improvised rings and reel and all was ready for the river. Den

Vaughan, Bertie Cahill and Denny Carthy may now enjoy their rewards for all that kindness and patience, but I hope that their purgatory was not lengthened for leading me on a course of distraction with fishing when serious work matters were left to wait.

It was from them that I learned how to fish with the artificial fly. Red Spinner, Greenwell's Glory, Wickham's Fancy, Hare's Ear and Alder got pride of place on the Dallow and Allow. Both streams had water of limestone quality and provided fine brown trout. It was agreed that good as the artificial fly was with the river flow at normal heights, nothing could beat the wood bee on a sunny day. This insect was of bluebottle size but with grey bars on its body. As its name suggests, it frequented trees and was readily drawn to fresh horse dung. When dapped into the eye of a whirlpool it was a deadly bait. It brought me the biggest trout I ever caught on the Allow: all of two pounds, at John's Bridge where O'Sullivan Beara forded on his way north to Leitrim after the Battle of Kinsale.

Later on I discovered that the place to be when the flood rose high was the Feale river, beyond Rockchapel around Thado's Cross. There was where the worm really came into its own when the sea trout, locally called white trout, were running. We would have our stock of blue-head worms nourished and hardened ready for action, knowing that time and tide wait for neither man nor boy. The fishing rod would have been strapped to the bar of the bike with the Wellingtons astride. Getting to that bike was the challenge as the school clock lumbered its slow uphill progress to three o'clock. All too often Master Jeremiah Browne would log on injury time to complete a lesson. He was a conscientious teacher, one not inclined to indulge our predominant passion for fishing. Right or wrong we read this expression of a conscientious work ethic as a policy with purpose aforethought, an exquisite way of reining in our juvenile impulses. Of course it had the opposite effect. By the time we got through the school door those impulses would have been ratcheted up to white heat by the anticipation born of enforced delay. The run west would have been close enough to ten miles over pot-holed roads. Stephen Roche and Sean Kelly would have been proud of us as we ate up the distance. By the time we arrived at the front prepared for action the choice spots would have been taken by the old stagers who well knew the lies the sea trout favoured. They did not give much leeway to the Meelin expeditionary force.

You might find space at the tail end of the pool where two streams joined near Thado's Cross. That represented a trap for the innocent angler. Planted there was an old bedspring ready to snag the Blue Devon or the Lane Minnow of the unwary, typically us Corkmen ignorant of Kerry wiles. However, we learned quickly. It was said that come the morrow with the spate past, a local would drop by on-spec for any by-product of the flood. In the war years some of those metal baits were almost worth their weight in silver.

So many happy associations come home to roost as one glides down memory lane. The cuckoo calling; the corncrake rasping; the jacksnipe whirring on leaving the river bank at dusk. As one looks back one recalls the exclamation of that prince of fishermen Izaak Walton in *The Compleat Angler* of three and a half centuries ago: 'I'll tell you, scholar: when I sat last on this primrose bank, and looked down these meadows, I thought of them as Charles the Emperor did of the city of Florence: that they were too pleasant to be looked upon, but on holy-days.'

Looking back on those times one appreciates the total sense of security and freedom that we enjoyed. Certainly parents must have been uneasy about the dangers we might encounter in our activities. The bank of a river high in flood is not a safe place for a keen young angler. True enough, but they must have felt that our guardian angels or the neighbours would keep an eye on us. Neighbourly concern for everyone's well-being was taken for granted in what was a genuine, caring community, before sociologists ever analysed the concept of

Gesellschaft/Gemeinschaft, society/community. No one then contemplated the sense of danger which parents feel today when they allow children out of sight.

It reminds one of the gospel story of Jesus rambling off from his parents on the way home from Jerusalem. No panic. He will be away with the friends or neighbours. On our outings to Priory Wood that must have been how relaxed our parents felt. There was no need for the warning signs *Community Alert* and *Pobal ar Aire*. There was no one to fear. It was unquestionably an ideal environment for child rearing. Children could push out the frontiers for developing skills of independent living without any overpowering sense of need for a safety harness.

Around the same time as Izaak Walton, Dr Samuel Johnson in his famous dictionary saw anglers as idle good-for-nothings. He described the fishing rod as a stick with a worm at one end and a fool at the other! In this he was devoid of soul and failed to appreciate that angling is more than just catching fish. Izaak Walton spoke for all of us in addressing 'brothers of the angle'. The patience is far from boring. You may catch a few fish, but that is indeed a bonus. Listening to the stream and feeling in tune with nature is balm for the soul. 'Éist le glór na habhann agus geobhair breac.' (It may also be the way to catch fish.) Perhaps, but there is more to it.

What I have described above about life would have been the general experience in the rural Cork of the time. It is well reflected in Alice Taylor's *To School Through the Fields*. Her Lisrobin is not that far southwest of Meelin. However, Meelin had one unique feature: the limestone quarries around which the village had developed. This stone industry identified and gave character to the little village.

– THE STONE QUARRIES –

The blue flint limestone was in particular demand for buildings where long-term weathering was the main concern. It qualified as freestone without the layering typical of limestone. It was dense as granite and would withstand water penetration and the frost which caused 'shelling' in lesser quality limestone. Church spires and quay walls would employ it to last out long years of exposure. Gravestones of Meelin limestone are still free of lichen after two centuries. It is still recalled that as the spire of Killarney Cathedral was being constructed in Meelin the stone was carted back overnight by a train of horses at £1 per load. Each horse hauled a ton. The train was headed by a steady animal who would set the pace to get the distance, close on thirty miles. The typical horse at that time was the Irish Draught, in much demand today for breeding hunter-class foals from thoroughbred sires. Horses travel better at night. They would be given a day to rest up in Killarney while another team already rested would face the return journey.

The flawless block of polished limestone serving as holy water font in the porch of Meelin church shows the quality of the marble material and the skill of the stonecutters. The famed sculptor Seamus Murphy did his apprenticeship in Meelin. His book *Stone Mad* is a mine of information on his time there and on the culture of the work shed. One of his jobs as apprentice was drawing cans of porter to 'cut the dust' for the line of stonecutters at work along the bench.

Where did all those thousands of tons of cut stone eventually go? Imagine the specialised work that went into shaping and facing each stone! Some certainly are still where they were fitted first day. Other structures were knocked down and buried to form the foundations of later buildings. The stones from the army barracks in Buttevant provided the foundation for the terraces of the GAA pitch there. At least they remain safe, to be retrieved in years to come when they may serve some nobler purpose. Mallow was glad to replace some worn limestone steps in the Parish Centre from those preserved in Buttevant.

By the time of my schooldays the stone quarries were no longer the busy places they had been in Seamus Murphy's day. Most of the limestone in use was now the softer quality from

Ballinasloe. Composite stone had replaced the natural as building material, and manual rock breaking for road metalling had ceased. The vast quarries were still there and those dizzy heights attracted the more daring among us to scale the stone faces. Our parents warned us off them as no-go areas. The force of that warning was endorsed by the unpredictable Jim Tobin. He lived beside the most accessible of the quarries and was reputed to take direct action against marauding youngsters. I regret now that we did not get to hear his life story. He was the local entrepreneur who had tried his luck at manufacturing mineral water in pressurised glass-stoppered bottles, which would now be worth good sums as antiques. One surmises that the reason for the failure of that enterprise was that the returnable bottles were not returned. The imprisoned glass marbles used as stoppers proved too much of an attraction to school boys. When he changed his line of business to the manufacture of boot polish the 'factory' burned down in a great conflagration of the flammable raw materials. The gaunt ruin like some blighted Hellfire Club kept us at a safe distance.

If Jim Tobin was unapproachable he was the exception. The few remaining resident stonecutters and other tradesmen held open house for us youngsters. The tradesmen had enjoyed good business in the era of quarry working when up to a hundred workers could be on site. The village then became self-sufficient in servicing the quarry operation.

Beside the school was Patsy the Tailor. If you read Eric Cross's *The Tailor and Ansty* you will get the picture. Patsy sat crosslegged by his bench repairing working clothes and making the odd pair of heavy-duty trousers. He was always ready to lay down the needle and entertain us with stories: actual or invented did not matter. Meanwhile Annie stoked the turf fire and had little to say bar a cackle of a laugh now and then.

When it came to real storytelling Jer Collins, a self-employed stonecutter, was your man. He always had a great welcome for us and, when in the humour, our questions would get him going with explanations and anecdotes. What a shame that we did not record them for posterity! The late John Joe Brosnan, a friend of my schooldays and a fine journalist in his. own right, certainly did take down an amount of material from local characters on a wire recorder. Whether or not the archive will ever be transcribed depends on how decipherable it still is.

I cannot leave this area without referring to the forge. The skill of the smith in tempering chisels was crucial for working the hard Meelin limestone. Today the production of tungsten-tipped instruments has displaced the steel tempering process of yesteryear. Science has replaced art. In the days before molecular research had revealed the secrets of the tempering process the Meelin smith knew how to achieve results through working ordinary mild steel. Smiths were ever credited with magical powers. In the hardening and tempering of raw iron one can see why. It all depended on the special method of forging through reading the alternating colours of the metal in the process of tempering.

We often had the task of taking a horse to the forge to be shod. Here another skill of the smith would be on display: his gift as horse whisperer in calming a restive animal. This would be evident when a smith would be called on to drain an abscess deep in the hoof. Working into the 'drop' with that little curved scalpel must have been painful. It was a matter of quiet authority born of confidence in getting the desired result. As we grew to size we might be called on to sledge the hot iron on the anvil. This was a real achievement. If we measured up we might even be invited to help in the banding of a cart wheel at the special location in the quarry. It was great to hear the wood creaking tight as we poured water on the contracting iron band. Of such are memories made.

Smiths were credited with magical powers. The forge water in which the hot iron was dipped was famed for its curative properties, particularly for the removal of warts. Folklore tells of the power of a smith's curse. In rage at some wrong done to him he would grasp the sledgehammer and smite the raw anvil so that its dire message of revenge rang out across the countryside. People would cower in dread from what was known in Gaelic as the war cries of the anvil, *greatha an iniúna*.

Our Meelin smiths were gentle folk. One of them, Jeremiah Murphy, known as Jer the Smith, would climb Meelin Hill to play the bagpipes of a summer evening. It was a long way from *greatha an iniúna*! That music would envelop the village and the whole valley in its embrace. Then we had Neily Fitzpatrick. He improvised the first welding apparatus in the locality. It was powered by an old Ford V8 engine shackled to a marine generator. It was a miracle that it held together in the one piece. He was an eligible bachelor and the locals observed how girls would bring kitchen utensils quite frequently for repairs. Jer's son was authorised by Bord na gCapall as a farrier. He won many distinctions for his specialised skills in suiting horses with shoes. To a layman this may seem much-of-a-muchness but every thoroughbred has its own peculiarities which affect its form on the racecourse. Today a smith brings his forge with him in a specially adapted van. One day I had the good fortune to be given a lift in just such a van when my car broke down on the way to a formal meeting in Cork. I made an impressive entry as this strange chariot wound its way among the Mercs and Volvos.

– DOGS AND RABBITS –

I love dogs. I have loved them for as long as I can remember. As I write this I have my three Red Setters stretched on the ground around me – Dara, Deise and Cora. They are my familiars, charmed and charming, bewitched and bewitching as they reflect the *genius loci* of ancient campfires. For the little they require in terms of bed and board they return one hundredfold in affection and loyalty. The house would be a vacant anonymous building without them. They inspire so many happy memories and carry so many associations with friends of times past. I realise that, at seventeen years, the old warrior Dara is on borrowed time. That is the downside of having a long-lived favourite dog. The French philosopher Thoreau commented that one difference between him and his dog was simply that the dog did not know that it would die.

Anyway, let us put these morbid thoughts to one side, as happy memories come to mind. On a farm one is fond of dogs but it is not sentiment. These are working dogs, not pets: partners in the day's work. They enjoy their role and know that they are appreciated for a job well done. That team spirit has been built up through the thousands of years since first Stone Age man trained up wolf cubs to help in the hunt. Around the campfires they shared the food and sensed themselves a part of the family pack.

Really to understand the man–dog relationship one should watch a pair of dogs herding sheep down from a rocky mountain in Kerry. The man stands below where he can survey the whole field of action. With whistles and hand signals he directs one or other dog to individual sheep hidden in the rough terrain. The dogs then marshall them all into a flock and sweep in any mavericks. When the man closes the corral gate each dog gets a pat on the head. For them that says it all. You can see it in their eyes as they look up at him. A dog of that quality is priceless, not for sale at any sum.

At home we would have a sheepdog for bringing in the cows. In fact I recall one particular dog so keen on the task that at a word he would take off to the fields on his own. On a wet morning this was surely welcomed. Strangely enough, I do not recall any dogs at home dying of old age. They certainly would not be put down just because they could no longer work. My father was a sensitive man and fond of his animals. In his mind horses were entitled to die on the land which they had worked all their lives. Perhaps dogs at that time were not long-lived in the absence of vaccinations against the diseases then prevalent. In any case I have little memory of individual sheepdogs. They have all blurred into one black and white. This is certainly not so where terriers and lurchers come into the picture. The reason for this is simply because these were partners in the hunt for rabbits. For my brother Tom and for me there was nothing to beat this. In the days before myxomatosis rabbits were everywhere. Indeed only for our efforts and those of our colleagues they might have taken over the land! If the Pied Piper once rid Hamelin of its plague of rats, we released Meelin and its environs from the fear of being eaten out of house and home by rabbits. Not that, as we will soon explain, the campaign won general gratitude from farmers.

Dogs were very effective partners in the rabbit campaign. The terriers were the shock troopers. When the going got tough the tough got going. Blackthorn, briar, bramble, furze were taken in their stride by terriers as par for the course. No matter where a rabbit had entrenched itself they charged in regardless. Their courage was unquestioned. I still picture a small terrier tangling with a dog fox in deep cover. As the fox broke out the terrier held him in a vice grip by the hind leg as he was dragged tumbling across a field. Another terrier showed marked cunning when a hound was in pursuit of a hare in a field of rushes. From previous experience the terrier knew about the usual escape route and would make a beeline to head the hare off at the gate.

In my young days I heard of a group from Newmarket who had trained a team of three terriers to hunt rats in the Dallow river under Clonfert. One terrier would hold the river, treading water when necessary, while his mates scoured the banks. Once a rat was flushed into the stream all three took to the water. As one dog tired the team would change places. A question remains. How were the dogs trained in the first place to hold their particular stations? However, for real intelligence the lurcher was the one. Crossbred he might be but here was no stupid mongrel. The lurcher was traditionally the poacher's dog, generally a cross between hound and sheepdog or hound and setter. The secret was to combine the speed of the one with the wit of the other. Very early after the pups in the litter had opened their eyes an expert would note the one on the move exploring its surroundings. That would mark out its potential for the future. At least it marked out evidence of lively interest and intelligence. Speed would have to be proved later in the field.

The lurcher would be quick to learn from experience. A foolish impetuous dog would have charged through a furze brake barking and yowling while the rabbit ran free away out the far side. Not so your intelligent lurcher. He would make a token charge with a bark or two and then skip around the back to meet the rabbit on the way out. If the rabbit got ahead across a field the dog would keep his distance waiting for the rabbit to check his run as he slowed down to creep into the burrow. The lurcher would have learned that a rabbit cannot drive in at speed as a train would into a tunnel.

On the ways of rabbits we were experts. We knew how to breed and rear ferrets, keeping the buck away from the doe in case he would eat the young kits. We had terriers trained up to pinpoint the location of a ferret if he went to ground in a warren. Today's ferreters employ a radio device for the purpose. Then as now farmers were not happy if we dug out a fence to retrieve a ferret, however much they appreciated our work in controlling the rabbit population. It was a twenty-four hour operation. At night we had snares planted on the runs. At first sight this might seem an easy way of catching rabbits. Far from it. The where and how required hard-won expertise to achieve success. At fall of night, if the dogs were still lively after a hard day, we would be out with a battery-powered beam to dazzle rabbits that had moved out into the fields.

Nowadays most people would read all this as a blood sport and see us as bloodthirsty killers. I must submit a correction for the sake of balance. This was not arbitrary killing for the sake of killing. There was really not exclusive emphasis on the sport side either. This was not just business for pleasure. This was business for profit. At that time during the war years of the forties rabbits sold at around four and five to the pound. That was a bonanza. A pound then was a serious amount of money. Today it would rate at thirty euros at least in its buying power.

Still, in hindsight, I do now have qualms about the cruelty involved. In this more sensitive climate it is clear that bloodsports have had their day. Even though I still have my Red Setters I no longer shoot. The memories still live on of the Glorious Twelfth, the opening of the grouse season on 12 August. Many a morning back on Muisire at dawn we would mark down the location of the packs by the giveaway crowing of the old cock grouse. Now, the very thought of killing grouse, pheasant or woodcock chills me. They are such glorious birds and so much at home in their natural environment. The change of heart for me came quite suddenly some years ago as a cock pheasant in all his shining pride launched himself on a frosty morning from under a holly bush. What a sight! Much to the dismay of the dog I dropped the gun from my shoulder. That was it.

I know that some will charge me with inconsistency because I am still addicted to the fishing rod. In justification I could invoke Scripture on the experience of Jesus with the Apostles. Fair point. To add to that, if you want to eat fish someone must catch them either commercially or for sport. A number of people will accept the former but not the latter. Well, are they then more concerned about the pleasure gained by the angler in pitting his wits against the wiles of the fish than about the pain suffered by the fish as it is brought to the net? Anyway fish are anonymous and lack individuality. An old warrior of a cock pheasant has personality. He owns his territory and is entitled to it. Why turn him into a heap of feathers? Finally, as years go by I have become more and more conservationist. If I catch a really fine fish now, I admire and slip him back into the water. There are enough of lesser specimens to pass muster for the frying pan.

– EARLY TO SCHOOL –

My grandfather, Denny O as he was known, taught me my ABC from a Land League slogan on the coping of the bridge beside my home in Meelin. It contained strong words about boycotting the grabber in the context of a local eviction. The political meaning did not carry a message for me then. It was the spelling that counted and that spelling stood out loud and clear. Unlike scrawled graffiti of today every letter was then perfectly crafted as in the copperplate style practised in national schools of that time. Shortly after my ABC initiation I went to Meelin National School at the age of three and a half. There I got a solid grounding which stood me well into the future. The teachers in the boys' school were Christina Barry and Jeremiah Browne. I have nothing now but happy memories of both. Then, I suppose, there must have been some testing times when I had omitted homework or lacked attention in class. Anyway, our wayward doings and omissions do not seem to have shortened the lives of our teachers. As I write this Master Browne, as he is still known, has already celebrated his hundredth birthday. He has provided me with that background on Meelin's National School and on the hedge school tradition of the locality, all in flawless copperplate style.

In the culture of the time teachers were really respected. Inside the school, discipline certainly ruled. Any deliberate disturbance of the even tenure of the school programme was not tolerated. Any physical punishment would have been moderate enough but the fear was that the story would carry home with further reprisals to come. In those days parents rarely second-guessed teachers in the discipline stakes. If they were partisan they might fear that they would simply move the problem down the line and have themselves dealing with it later.

One now regrets the prevalence of corporal punishment as incentive to learning. The Irish proverb gives a better slant on the educational process. *Mol an óige agus tiochfaidh sí* (Praise the youth and it will flourish). Approval of one's efforts achieves more than disapproval of one's shortcomings. Taking the stick to pupils who had learning problems engendered a dislike of school. Hence a vicious circle. Shakespeare's description of the schoolboy comes to mind: 'crawling like snail unwillingly to school.' Many have carried a grievance with them through life, particularly where that is bolstered with a sense of unfairness.

Today we have gone full circle where teachers feel that disapproval of a pupil's poor efforts may injure his self-esteem. This unbalanced system does a disservice to the pupil. It is poor preparation of character for life. Life is a tough taskmaster and gives little quarter to those who try to compete on false premises. It quickly scrapes off the tinsel of inflated self-estimation. In everything the Golden Rule should apply. *Virtus in medio stat* – good sense strikes a balance between extremes.

Thinking of teachers who got the balance right, one man comes to mind: Bryan McMahon of Listowel. He tells the story of his life in that book *The Master*. He and John B. Keane lived side by side. Each stimulated the other as writer. Both were gifted to an extraordinary degree. From the book one can picture Bryan McMahon as the superb teacher he undoubtedly was. One sees him as a type of Socrates firing the imagination and inspiring lateral thinking. A born teacher, yet he was not the kind to indulge his pupils. He got respect because he expected it of them. He had the personality to impress and carry conviction. I do not recall whether he used the cane on the recalcitrant, but I doubt it.

During a discussion in the course of the Listowel Writers' Week some years back the life of the schoolteacher came up for analysis. Naturally Bryan McMahon gave a good account of his personal experience. He spoke of how much the teaching of pupils had been fulfilling and stimulating for him. It was evident that for him schooldays were among the best days of his life. Today the life of a teacher is far more of a challenge than in his time. What a torture it must be to face in day after day where one is discontented and reduced to seeing the role as a job, an unwelcome one at that.

Whatever about a job in business or industry the work of a teacher who lacks a personal sense of achievement must leave him or her emotionally drained and derelict. In days past, teaching was at least tolerable because there was an effective system of discipline. Still, one wonders how many teachers may have visited excessive physical punishment on pupils because of a festering discontent with their lot in life. The problem today is that teachers are left helpless in face of the trouble occasioned by disruptive pupils. It must be stressed that other pupils – and their teachers – have rights which call for respect in their place of work and study. Currently this issue needs to be addressed as a matter of priority.

Once a garda pulled me over for breaking the speed limit on entering a town. It actually was on that stretch between the two halves of Rathmore. I accepted that I was guilty as charged. As he produced the book to write the summons he could not come up with his pen. I reached into the car and handed him mine. He looked at it, shook his head and handed it back. His father, he said, had been sent out by a teacher to cut a stick to punish himself and he had carried the grievance to his dying day. It was one time when another's grievance served me well as I got off with a caution.

In my days at school, teachers were held in great respect by the community at large outside the school. They were recognised for their quality of leadership in the parish and for their place in inculcating and endorsing an accepted system of values. Bryan McMahon speaks of the teacher as leaving the track of his teeth on three generations. The triumvirate of Parish Priest, Master and Garda stood shoulder to shoulder in dealing with any problem that came the way. I remember a visit to the school by the Garda Sergeant in full uniform investigating a spate of breakages of conductor 'bottles' on telephone poles along the Meelin–Newmarket line. The Sergeant made his official complaint and spelled out the sanction. It was left to the Master, who had quickly built up a *prima facie* list of suspects, to root out the miscreants responsible.

They were innocent times at school when the only infringement of law and order that I can call to mind was that boyish prank. Schooldays for me were happy, all the happier because they were so much part of that full life which I have already described. In his oath governing the behaviour of physicians Hippocrates, the ancient Greek master of medical science, directs that apprentice physicians show utmost respect for their mentors. Amen to that. What I learned in study method in Meelin National School put down a solid foundation. Nothing could have substituted for that.

It was Master Browne who chose William Bulfin's *Rambles in Eirinn* as reading matter for our senior year at school. It was an inspired choice. The book traced the author's leisurely travels on a bicycle through rural Ireland early in the last century. It was a cornucopia of information giving items of history and geography in a human dimension right across the land. Bulfin's heart and mind burned with patriotic fervour. He certainly fired our imaginations with his stories of exploits of old on hill and dale. His was a quiet voice but all the more persuasive for that. As life goes forward the strident manifesto tends to grate. It just reminds one of the fire-and-brimstone preacher who would add a marginal comment to his sermon notes, 'Argument weak, shout!' I hope that *Rambles in Eirinn* is still in print after its first publication in 1907. My current copy dates from 1981. I often take it up in a moment of reverie. Its magic never dates. For that I thank Master Browne.

– FOOD FOR MIND AND HEART –

Once I had basic reading skills under my belt the world of books opened a door that has never closed. The first book I got to read at home was Kenneth Grahame's *The Wind in the Willows*. I think it was given to me by my grandfather as a present after my first few weeks in school. With his help I worked my way through it. I needed little motivation to get on with reading after that.

Kenneth Grahame appealed to the imagination of anyone drawn to country lore. He introduced me to a Victorian world of fantasy where badger, rat, mole, toad and their neighbours had assumed their specific personalities as they plied the Thames and its backwaters. It was a charmed world and it certainly bewitched me. Years later as priest on a visit to Reading I prevailed on a friend to drive us down to Pangbourne-on-Thames where Kenneth Grahame had composed the book. It was a magical place. The willows still trailed lazily in the water beside the wooden deck of the pub where, with his pint of plain, the author had sat reflecting on the passing scene. I am glad that his book continues in print and still holds the attention of children young and old, generation after generation. The book is now available on BBC Audio books acted out in a selection of voices by Sir Derek Jacobi. That well-presented version is hard to fault. Still, for me at any rate, a CD cannot replace the written word.

Even though it was a work of fantasy it gave a special dimension to the lore of the countryside by providing personalities for the various animals. The language was also well crafted with a poetic quality. Unless there is some poetic quality in language or some real insight into human nature I find that novels have little attraction. I fear that sentiment, well described as false or unearned emotion, leaves me cold. The books that I read by choice are of a historical or scientific nature where one can follow evidence and analyse an argument. Documentaries always hold attention. In 1950 the first Penguin books were published. These I then treasured at prices a student could afford. The enterprising Penguin publisher, Allen Lane, deserves the gratitude of the generations of young people who came to appreciate well researched and well written books.

I am never more happy than with a book. Even though I favour those with historical or scientific content, any book of fiction written with style and with appeal to the imagination will do. Like many boys of the time I would have read Robert Louis Stephenson's *Treasure Island*. What an imaginative gift he had for holding us spell-bound! Even that obituary on his South Sea tombstone reflects that quality of his: 'Here he lies where he longs to be. Home is the sailor home from the sea and the hunter home from the hill.' Then there was that extraordinary mixture of fact and fiction in Daniel Defoe's *Robinson Crusoe*. It all came back to me recently when I read of the discovery of six hundred barrels of pirate gold on the Juan Fernandez Island in the South Seas where Alexander Selkirk (Defoe's Robinson Crusoe) had spent those long years as a castaway not suspecting that he walked over such a treasure.

Documentaries on nature at first hand have always claimed attention. Eamonn de Buitléir and Gerrit van Gelderen are gifted both as observers and writers. I find a book describing what an adventurer observes even more interesting than the camera shot. The book gives the writer's impressions and appeals to the imagination. Some gifted writers weave a scene in words which carry magic in their power to evoke feeling for nature. The books of Laurens Van der Post transport one into the eloquent silence of the South African veldt as the Southern Cross hangs glittering in the sky.

In the philosophy of the ancients, poetry writing was seen as inspired by the muses. It was a preternatural gift. Whatever about that, it is certainly a very special talent over and above the ordinary run of human imagination. Beside my bed I keep a book of Seamus Heaney's *Collected Poems*. Seamus Heaney inspires me not only by his insights into human nature but by his skill in finding just the right expressions. I picture him pen in hand as his mind runs along promising veins of language.

One is reminded of that ancient Irish scribe at his writing desk. 'I and Pangur Ban my cat, 'tis a like task we are at. Chasing mice is his delight, hunting words I spend all night.' This is what inspires poetry. No wonder the ancients saw a muse at work. The glory of Seamus Heaney is that he invests ordinary down-to-earth experiences with new depths of meaning. I am sure that he works hard at finding just the right expression but it seems to come so naturally to him. The Latin proverb says it well: *Ars est celare artem*. There is art in hiding craft. A poem of his titled 'The Haw Lantern' is a good example. Observing a single haw holding out on a thorn bush into late winter leads him to a parable on life. He sees that challenging haw as reflecting the action of the ancient Greek philosopher Diogenes who circulated with his lantern through Sicily searching for one honest man.

Patrick Kavanagh has a similar gift of poetic genius but there is a darker quality to it. 'O stony grey soil of Monaghan you burgled my bank of youth.' Kavanagh threw off poems without putting much work in the polishing. He was prodigal with a talent which promised much more than he achieved on the page. Kavanagh's 'Raglan Road', a favourite song of the late Luke Kelly, showed that depth of genius, a potential that brought one to wish for more as the words flowed all too easily. His brother Peter, a professor of English in America, collected and published everything he wrote. It was not the right decision. There are diamonds there among the rubble but that rubble takes from the effect. Alan Warner's book *Clay is the Word* shows what a poet Patrick Kavanagh was. He may have thrown off some of his poetry in double quick time but at that they may strike fire as flashes of pure genius.

Seamus Heaney, with such imagination and gift of language, must have been a source of inspiration for his students in coming to appreciate the world of literature. He is rooted far back in the Greek and Latin classics and in the Old English of Beowolf. The ideas he uses, apparently so simple on the surface, have frequently been refined and honed by minds and hearts of philosophers and poets for generation after generation. He brings them down to a level where we can appreciate them as personal experiences.

To our scientific and technological cast of mind the ancients may seem primitive and outdated when measured against the results of our projects in research and development. We must never forget that in the spiritual world of human imagination the ancients may have been just as advanced as we are, possibly more so because they had few distractions. Those who observe the drawings and paintings of now extinct animals etched by Stone Age man in the caves of the Dordogne region on the frontier of France and Spain stand in awe of the human imagination. It might be just a rough sketch of the deer glancing back as the hunters arrive in hot pursuit. Still it holds today's observer in silent attention with its timeless message. How do you feel when you see the footprints left by a Stone Age man and his dog etched on the soft ground in the interior of a cave! As the Psalmist says in the Bible: 'Heart speaks to heart.'

It is in this sense that there is something timeless about great literature. That is why Homer, Virgil and Shakespeare remain contemporary. What they have to say about human nature stands the test of time in this unbroken chain of poetic imagination. Writers and poets convey to us insights which vibrate from a distance but still preserve their freshness in the mind that now captures them on the page. Maybe I am a philistine about much of what now passes as contemporary art, music and poetry. One has the feeling that where something is so outrageous that it stops people open-mouthed in their tracks it may well pass as art. Take that instalment of an unmade bed with paraphernalia scattered around on the floor. Then that series of tin cans containing human excrement, one of which was bought by Britain's Tate Gallery to add to its collection of modern art! Even though normal people are indignant and disgusted most are slow to criticise, in case a large sum of money at auction might qualify something as 'art'.

It was a relief to read an article in *The Sunday Times* of 22 May 2005 by its art critic John Carey on 'What is a Work of Art?' In a word he concluded that where contemporary art is concerned there are no objective criteria. To the question: 'Is it a work of art?' all one can say is, 'Yes, if you think it is; no, if not'. So, on that test, I am prepared to dismiss out-of-hand, as the rubbish I believe them to be, what often passes as art and those tinsel pop songs which have nothing worthwhile to say in terms of either words or music. Repetition of the same shallow themes in the so-called lyrics tries the patience. If something is not worth saying once it certainly is not worth saying twice and again and again. What comes to mind is that parable of the child who blurts out to the sycophantic courtiers that the mad Emperor, whose apparel they profess to admire, is not wearing any clothes! One may conclude that much of what passes as modern art may well reflect a culture of nihilism, where a sense of meaninglessness and alienation rule OK.

Anyone who has heard of Socrates knows that he upheld as absolutes 'The Good, the True and the Beautiful'. These, he said, exist in a sphere outside that of human experience, in the World of Ideas. This ideal world qualifies as real for him. His disciple Plato spells out its implications in the Parable of the Cave. In this life we are as it were gathered in a cave with the sun's light behind us. On the back wall of the cave our shadows and those of others are moving along. This relative world that we experience is a shadow land, a reflection of the perfect World of Ideas.

The German philosopher Immanuel Kant in his *Critique of Judgment* followed along similar lines in setting out his theory on aesthetics. For him, standards of beauty were fixed as absolute and universal. Those standards have been ingrained in the human mind and in the human imagination, to a greater or lesser degree depending on one's sensitivity. There was a kind of sixth sense which perceived what Socrates defined as 'The Good, the True and the Beautiful'. This artistic sense could be trained and refined to inspire a consensus as to what was genuine art.

Art evaluation is not an exact science like mathematics. Still it moves across a discernible spectrum as a barometer moves in charting the weather. Given that spectrum one can see why the *Venus de Milo* and Michelangelo's *Pietà* strike us as fine art and why Homer and Shakespeare rate as great literature. Fine art and great literature have their seeds as ideas in the sculptor's or writer's rich imaginations. It is then a matter of creating the medium to communicate the idea to the observer or to the reader. Michelangelo puts this concept across very neatly in his sculpture *The Prisoners*. At first sight it looks unfinished. He explained that he has been releasing his mental image from the encasing marble block. He had done enough for the observer to do the rest for himself by imaging the finished work.

As for music I cannot sing a note, even though I may batter the ears of any group once the craic is good in a come-all-ye session. In Maynooth I would resignedly address the plain Gregorian chant as I presided in turn at Solemn Sunday Mass. When asked by the organist what note I would take for the *Gloria in excelsis Deo* I would have been tempted to say, as one colleague had done to our great amusement: 'I am not a prophet!' Plain chant did assist the indifferent singer but I doubt that even that measured down to my level.

Even so I love to listen to traditional music and to any form of *bel canto*. As for what rates in the pop charts for me today it all adds up to heavy metal, *can belto*. I accept that it has a huge following, in particular among young people. Is it a form of escapism, much like drug taking, which wafts audiences into a world of virtual reality rather than confront the pressures of life?

Anyway I can never thank enough those teachers who introduced us to the world of books. What a lifelong gift they conferred on us! As I write on style in literature and art I fear that I come over as conceited and opinionated. That I would regret, and would apologise for the impression. Later on when I came to study theology, the absence of any style in the writing became a barrier. Fair enough, one expects and respects the need for technical terminology. Otherwise accurate meaning cannot be conveyed. Beyond that, what is surely required is personal colour in language and expression so that the meaning shines out afresh. Unfortunately, most theological treatises are heavy and turgid. Authors forget form as they over-concentrate on content. 'Words are like leaves and where they most abound much fruit of sense beneath is rarely found.' How often a well thought-out and well-written article in a theological journal will expand into a laboured book, adding nothing except words to the original.

CHAPTER 2

THE ROAD TO PRIESTHOOD

Looking back I appreciate how deeply spiritual was the culture in which we grew up in the Ireland of the time. That word 'spiritual' is preferable to 'religious'. Where the stress is on religion it may reflect a dour attachment to ritual formulae and practices. For us, spirituality was really celebrating day-to-day Christian life and religion was part of that. Being Christian and Catholic certainly did not stand in the way of being human. Sociologists and historians criticise the Irish Catholicism of the past as being oppressive and obscurantist. At its upper echelons the Church of the time may have been authoritarian, given to protecting the position of power and prestige with which history had endowed it. That institutional Church was at a safe distance for us in Meelin. In rural Ireland people lived their faith pretty much as they always had done. It pervaded their culture and gave meaning to their lives. There was generally great respect for the priests in the parish. This reflected the affection for the *sagart aroon* which traced back to when the local priests had stood with their people in the harsh times of the *drochshaol*. This was the actual Church. The institution to which the media refer was some kind of virtual Church.

Unquestionably there were priests, particularly some parish priests, who were grasping and dictatorial. This minority provided the stereotype for much Irish writing of a later age. Indeed it may have been the clash with such a figure that

45

inspired many a strong character to take up the pen and dip it in vitriol! One recalls the treatment meted out to Brinsley McNamara of *The Squinting Windows* and John McGahern of *The Dark*. I have since felt that one writer who gave the most balanced and least rancorous account of the priest in rural Ireland was the late John B. Keane. Anyway, the priests in Meelin of my time were down-to-earth pastors and regarded highly in the community.

There was an atmosphere of prayer in the home in which I grew up. That would have been typical of the time. Before we ever went to school we would have learned the pattern of morning and evening prayers. On most evenings the family Rosary would have been said. Aspirations on meeting someone in passing came spontaneously as suited the occasion. 'God bless the work'; 'It's a terrible day, thank God'; 'God bless you and yours.' When I later read that extraordinarily rich collection of blessings and aspirations garnered from Gaelic sources by the Jesuit An t-Athair Diarmuid O'Laoghaire I could see that some of it had still been preserved in our day-to-day exchanges. However, in my youth many of the daily litany of blessings and aspirations which would have come so readily to former Gaelic speakers were no longer current – blessings on hearing the cock crow, on lighting the fire, on starting the day's work, on seeing the moon rise, on raking the fire and much else.

Still, the background survived. I recall the blessing of the crops with holy water on Ember Days. When a heifer had her first calf my father would light the blessed candle and singe her udder to secure a good milking. I wonder now whether that was a ritual charm to protect against the evil eye. Belief in pisheogs was well established at the time. Eggs in cocks of hay or in the potato garden boded ill. It was perceived as evidence that some evil-minded person had purposed to do injury or to steal the produce. There were stories of approaches to the priest to celebrate Mass to ward off the malice. The priests would not favour this belief in superstition or in charms or spells. Neither did they campaign against it as they certainly had done in earlier times when pisheogs would have been common practice. The files in the Vatican from the first meetings of the *Congregatio de Propaganda Fide* in the early 1600s provide evidence that black magic was commonplace in Ireland from earlier times. The Sheila-na-Gig emblem found as frontispiece in many ancient churches was a charm to neutralise the evil eye, as is its more sanitised and stylised version in our horseshoe. The belief in superstition died away in face of more scientific knowledge of infection and contagion.

Prayer life in our young days reflected a general sense of trust in God's providence. Around the house the array of holy pictures would remind us that we were in God's hands. The picture of Consecration of the Family to the Sacred Heart was given pride of place in the kitchen. In the bedroom where my brother Tom and I slept there was a picture of the Guardian Angel directing a child over a rickety bridge. We would pray 'O Angel of God, my guardian dear, to whom God's love commits me here, ever this day be at my side to light and guard, to rule and guide. Amen'. Then you had the statue of the Blessed Virgin. Later when I came to read the life of Peig Sayers of the Great Blasket I appreciated how central Mary was to popular devotion in times of distress. She tells of her feelings as neighbours brought in the body of her drowned son and how she could not have taken on the task of laying out the body without the support of Mary, Mother of Sorrows. She took the statue down from its niche and placed it beside her on the kitchen table. She would then have felt close to Mary at the foot of the Cross where she too had received the body of her dead Son.

Thank God, in our home in Meelin we were not visited with that level of anguish. There was little call to appeal to Mary as Mother of Sorrows. The statue would have bided its time on the kitchen window until it was taken down on May Eve as we prepared to set up the May Altar. That May Altar carries happy memories for me still. I have never got around to tracing the origins of the devotion. I suspect that it is a particular Irish tradition and may be part of the usage which established May as the Month of Mary, replacing the pagan associations of Bealtaine, the Fire of Baal. The May Altar links firmly in my memory with the hymn of the Hypridean tenor Fr Sydney McEwan: 'O Mary, We Crown Thee With Blossoms Today.' With a heart and a half we met his invitation: 'Bring flowers of the rarest, bring blossoms the fairest.' Tradition gave choice of place to wild flowers as against garden varieties. Blue and white were preferred as Mary's colours. Hyacinths, cowslips, primroses, forget-me-nots were ideal.

At first sight the hawthorn, known in other parts of Ireland as the May Bush, should surely qualify. There was, however, a definite ban on bringing hawthorn, particularly with a pink blush, into the home. It was said to be unlucky. Did this have some link with Christ's crown of thorns? Or was there that pagan factor of connection with the Good People? 'All around the thorn tree the Little People play, and men and women passing turn their heads away.' Here is something to serve as a research project for Transition Year students before the memories are lost.

The May Altar indicates how faith was woven into our lives both at home and school. At school the younger pupils would have gathered the wildflowers as they walked along the road. Later I learned how anomalous the religious ethos of the national school was. The national school system was generally established after Catholic Emancipation in 1829 by First Secretary Stanley to provide State aid for Catholic education. In principle or *de iure* the system was non-denominational but in practice or *de facto* it became denominational. The first Irish solution to an Irish question! Originally, to preserve the appearance of a non-denominational system, a card reading 'Religious Instruction' on one side would be displayed on the wall during the period set for catechism. I can just recall, in Meelin school I think, such a card on a school wall – even though by then the ritual of turning it back and forward had long gone out of use.

Where education in the Catholic faith was concerned, home, school and parish reflected a common ethos. What committed teachers we had in Christina Barry and Jeremiah Browne! The debate in recent years over school as a place for religious education and/or catechetical formation was not then relevant. Our teachers aimed to communicate their faith to us as a sacred trust. The Catechism was the universal mode of instruction. It was to be memorised, learned word perfect by rote or by heart, as the saying was. The clearest focus in catechetical teaching related to preparation for the sacraments, First Confession/Communion and Confirmation. These really were milestones in our religious and human progress, *rites de passage* as sociology would now know them. The Penny Catechism, which was our *vademecum* in national school, was an abridgement of the famous Butler Catechism. Mercier Press has recently printed a new edition. It is an amazing book compiled by a priest who had a profound knowledge of the Catholic faith and wide experience in how to communicate it to young and old. Dr James Butler, Archbishop of Cashel and Emly, composed his Catechism in 1777. It was later revised and enlarged in 1802 when it incorporated further teaching on the duties of citizenship. The concern was the social and political unrest occasioned by the French Revolution which affected Ireland in the Rising of 1798.

The 1802 Butler General Catechism was further revised in 1875 as a national catechism for the whole country. The influence of the Butler Catechism was spread by Irish emigrant priests and people to the United States, Canada, Australia and New Zealand. It inspired national catechisms in those lands and in some cases was adopted with little change. The Catechism in full edition published by Mercier Press is a remarkable document. True enough there are shortcomings in it. James Butler was educated in France and as a result he drew on sources outside the native Gaelic religious and spiritual tradition. This was certainly a loss. In his question-and-answer method he also tended to define deep theological concepts too sharply as if the ideas were cut-and-dried and black-and-white in expression. Of course, the method of memorising the texts with the expectation that understanding would come later was very much the practice of the time. Still and all it stood us well in our school days and I still wonder at its quality. What a name Archbishop Butler has left during his short life of just under fifty years!

For us boys, being trained as altar servers was an important step in our relationship with the parish. It brought us into personal contact with the priest. It gave us a privileged role in the eyes of the congregation at Mass. We took pride in knowing the Latin responses even though we recited the formulae with little or no understanding of the actual meaning. In our eyes that did not take from the significance. It may have added to the sense of mystery and the feeling of how special the Mass was.

In my case certainly being with the priests in their role at the altar focused my mind on becoming a priest. I expect that this is how vocation came to many like me. Of course, it was reinforced at home – not that any express words were ever spoken. My grandfather Denny O did make some oblique references to the Capuchin priests as 'great men'. His remarks would have registered. Years later in that diary which he had kept during his years in Australia as a young man I learned that he had been initiated into the Third Order in Sydney by a Capuchin priest. Later as a priest I grew very close to the Capuchins where I have a dear friend of happy angling memories, Fr Mark Coyle in the friary at Ard Mhuire in Donegal. Actually the Sliabh Luachra area on the Cork/Kerry border counted numerous men who had become Capuchin friars. Anywhere I travelled in the world I would seek out the hospitality of the Capuchins. I always felt at home with them. Denny O's words had made a lasting impression.

– ST COLMAN'S COLLEGE, FERMOY –

However, all that was well in the future as I was sent off to boarding school in St Colman's College in Fermoy. It was a bleak place during the war years in the forties. Rationing of food hit hard on us growing youngsters. Without the welcome parcels from home we would have been on iron rations. What made it bearable was the camaraderie amongst ourselves and the opportunities for sport, particularly handball and hurling. In those times, before free secondary education had swelled the ranks of those seeking advance to Third Level, the Leaving Certificate examination did not exert the pressure it would later do under the points system. Those of us who were seriously considering going forward to become priests in the Diocese knew that we needed a credible Leaving Certificate to qualify for Maynooth. In fact I think that the six of us who did go forward for the Diocese of Cloyne were among the leading ten in the Leaving Certificate class of that year in the College.

In St Colman's we had some excellent teachers who instilled in us a love of learning. I particularly liked languages and found Latin and Greek really attractive. Even though grammar and syntax could be dry and boring I began to appreciate that they were key to understanding the structure and style of language as literature. I suppose at first we did not see much point in learning Latin and Greek except as examination subjects. Those so-called classics were 'dead' languages. One of our teachers, James McNamara, 'Jimmy Mac', took time out to explain how basic Latin and Greek were to the whole of education and civilisation. His talk would then have been considered a 'free class' but what an enlightening one it must have been! In later years I appreciated better what he was about. So much of the English language traces back to its roots in the classics. It is there that most specialist names for plants and flowers are to be found. Law and medicine still speak that language at one remove. I recall with joy when at an inter-University debate in Maynooth one of our student teams trumped the opposition by being able to derive the origin of the motto of the City of Cork, *Statio bene fida carinis*: a safe anchorage for ships. He knew that it was an adaptation of Virgil's description of the bad experience of the Greek fleet marshalled outside Troy. He referred to the original text in the *Aeneid* which spoke of the unsafe anchorage off the island of Otygia as *Statio male fida carinis*. It is good to know that, particularly in the USA, universities are re-introducing Latin as key to understanding the shape of language.

If anyone should question the value of Greek and Latin they will find the answer in Jim O'Donnell's *Wordgloss*: *A Cultural Lexicon*. What a treasury this is in tracing the roots of both technical and everyday language with a light touch unusual in scholars of his quality. He sums up his concern: 'Few people now study Latin and Greek. In order to appreciate the loss that has to be made up one has only to reflect on how Greek and Latin suffuse the vocabularies of the traditional core disciplines – philosophy, law, medicine, history, geography, mathematics – and on how the newer disciplines like psychology, sociology, anthropology and linguistics develop their nomenclature from Latin and Greek roots.'

One of the most influential philosophers of modern times has been the Jesuit priest Fr Bernard Lonergan. He himself certainly would have qualified as the Universal Man of the classical tradition. He embraced all the disciplines – philosophy in all its forms, literature, history, mathematics, theology. He pronounced that the overall classical culture had become extinct. 'The clearest and neatest illustration of the breakdown of classical culture lies in the field of science.' Knowledge had become fragmented so that specialists came to know more and more about less and less. The man or woman who could turn mind to anything was no more. Their world had passed into history. We may grant that the polymath of universal classical culture is no more. Still, it is good to know that the various strands of that culture, including the Latin and Greek spheres of literature, still survive in spite of the dominance of modern science as the determinant of modern culture.

In the ancient Hippocratic Oath one of the pledges made was that a student should show respect to his teachers. This was a duty of *pietas*. It reflected the natural regard for those influences which have made us what we are. I now regret that we made life difficult for one or two teachers. They were given little or no quarter in class and, indeed, were allowed little opportunity to teach their subjects effectively. Looking back one realises that they must have lacked enough self-confidence to maintain order. We who were subject to a strict climate of discipline otherwise in the College then found an occasion to break out in a form of catharsis, a mode of liberation for our suppressed spirits. The situation would not have amounted to mayhem but it was a constant low level of disorder if not malicious as a form of bullying. We must have made the teacher's day a misery. One does not rest easy with the memory now.

The educational ethos in St Colman's College served us well later at Third Level. There was no spoonfeeding with the precise purpose of meeting examination requirements. To a large extent one got on with study on one's own under the general direction of the teachers. This was in marked contrast with the system in some other schools. There the analysing of past examination papers was the stock-in-trade in the Leaving Certificate class. These were dissected and studied so that students could familiarise themselves with the typical form and structure of questions. It was something of a grind-school policy. The examination results would reflect this intense preparation. However, at Third Level one was then thrown in at the deep end. One had to sink or swim in a new challenging educational environment. For students of St Colman's the change of climate was a natural progression.

Looking back on days in Fermoy one recalls the rough-and-tumble of a typical boys' school at the time. Sport had a major place in our lives. Inter-school competitions were red-letter events, particularly when some traditional rivals for the Harty Cup, such as St Flannan's in Ennis, entered the lists for the final. Although not a high achiever on the field of play I was an active participant. St Colman's was strictly a GAA school. On one occasion early in October of my final year with the staff away we organised a rugby match. It was the one occasion when I suffered a quite serious injury with a compound fracture of the ankle.

After hospitalisation with the leg in plaster I was sent back to Meelin to recuperate for the remainder of term. With the home comforts there one could hardly call it an enforced absence from college. In double quick time I was out on crutches with the shotgun on the trail of rabbits. As winter closed in I read everything I could lay hands on. Naturally the countdown to the gale day of the Leaving Certificate in the new year could not be ignored. I had the textbooks to hand and ready help from some of my classmates, particularly a neighbour, Liam Guerin from Freemount. The self-help approach to education in St Colman's already described now proved its value for me.

Those months at home provided a first-class opportunity for reading. It honed my appetite for knowledge of every kind. My mother had bought from some travelling salesman the ten volumes or so of Cassell's *Book of Knowledge*. It was an encyclopaedia covering topics on everything under the sun that shone to the far reaches of the British Empire. At the time I was not conscious of the jingoism of John Bull. The volumes were informative and well produced. When I returned to St Colman's I got to reading books in the students' library there. I suspect most of them had come through bequests from the collections of deceased priests. Among them were volumes on fishing, shooting and hunting. I was drawn to Walton's *The Compleat Angler* or Maxwell's *Wild Sports of the West* rather than to more improving works of literature. Many happy hours were spent in that library when bad weather confined us to barracks. One of the books which I digested was a collection of articles on wild birds written in *The Messenger*. The challenge was to identify them all on the ground at home.

– FURTHER STEPS ON THE ROAD –

My mind was already directed towards becoming a priest during my years in St Colman's College. Having come to know priests as an altar server was certainly a positive factor, and we had some fine priests in Meelin at the time. One whose overall lifestyle I admired was Fr Tom Glavin, curate in Meelin. He taught us altar servers to learn the English equivalents of the Latin responses. We welcomed his visits to the school because he had a good line in storytelling to illustrate points in the Bible and Catechism. For me there were other links.

As a beekeeper he introduced me to the ways of bees which I followed up in later life. He was also an angler of special skill with the wood bee, also called the wood fly, that grey-bodied fly much the size of a blue bottle. With this he was expert on the Dallow and Allow rivers in high summer when trout were hard to catch. With that background, being a priest seemed to have a lot going for it in human terms.

All this was confirmed for me when I came to know my cousin, Fr Phil Foley. He was ordained in 1942, shortly before I went to St Colman's College. I spent much of my summer holidays with him as he moved to various parishes around the diocese. He certainly represented for me everything that a priest should be. He had a spiritual outlook on life. That life centred on commitment to the ministry of the people in his pastoral care. His generous personality made this most effective through his natural easy capacity to build relationships and associations. What today would be seen as skills to be learned in the process of formation were for him second nature.

In those summer holidays there was never a dull moment. Phil Foley could turn a hand to anything in building and repairing. If a part was not available he would improvise. I think that if he were stranded like Robinson Crusoe on that desert island he would be in his element while he worked out ways to escape. I was his willing apprentice like that Man Friday. Then he was keen on field sports, particularly with gun and dog. I have happy memories of grouse shooting on Muisire and Barr-a-Carthainn. It would take a whole volume to detail those happy days with Fr Phil. He had felt at home in country parishes for all of his earlier appointments. The promotion to the post of Administrator in the mensal parish of Fermoy did not fit in with his personality and experience. He was not at home in administration and paper work. Being the man and priest he was he did not express reservations when Bishop John Ahern had appointed him to that post in a busy town parish. Phil Foley was not untypical among priests of the time when it came to skills for maintaining everything in the parish in running order. It was second nature to get the tools out and address the problem when some appliance failed to function. On the occasion of the Station Mass the advice of such a priest would be sought and given respect for his expertise on many items. He would have been particularly on call for guidance on pros and cons as the system of rural electrification rolled out through the country.

Today comparatively few priests are do-it-yourselfers. Many readily admit that wiring a plug would stretch their capacity. It was different fifty years ago. I spent much of my holidays from Maynooth in the parish of Carrigtwohill with Phil Foley. The parish priest was Dean Jack Ahern. When it came to skills in making and fixing the Dean was a professional. His workshop featured the most advanced technology of the time. Then he was recognised among the most knowledgeable of beekeepers with a state-of-the-art apiary. Again I was a willing apprentice and eventually received the highest accolade of being trusted to carry on with some project whenever he was called away.

This centring of attention on handcrafts may seem a distraction on the way to having one's vocation to priesthood confirmed. On the contrary. It added to my respect for priests.

It provided better appreciation of how these good conscientious priests lived a healthy fulfilled life in the round. On the pastoral front it gave them greater credibility with the people. Anyway, did not God choose a carpenter's workshop as home for Jesus?

Later it all stood me in good stead. In Maynooth as a student the woodwork and beekeeping operations were a counterpoise to academic studies. They were an effective antidote to ennui and mental tiredness. They focused the mind. One put in quality time in study at one's desk knowing that a project awaited completion on the workshop bench. There one honed the skills of lateral thinking which also helped in study. Those times spent with kindred spirits were happy hours. *Mens sana in corpore sano.*

Later when on the staff at Maynooth I would drop into the College workshops and see what was underway. As Maynooth went through the process of reconstruction there was plenty of discarded pitch pine. This beautiful wood serves ideally for any kind of internal work. It is no longer available from source in the same quality as formerly. Just look at our old church furnishings! At ceremonies in the Maynooth College Church I would find my eyes straying to follow the grain on the Irish oak choir stalls, which rivalled pitch pine in quality.

Master joiner during my years on the staff was Joe McArdle, now gone to the Lord. He was gifted at restoring and blending new with old. He loved that pitch pine. He didn't mind the 'flour', the powdered saw dust that the high speed tungsten circular blade would shower far and wide as I cut wood down to size for some project or other. May Jesus, raised in the home of a carpenter, make a place for him in heaven.

That hands-on experience of construction work later spared me anxiety when undertaking various building projects in Mallow. I appreciate that priests from a cloistered background find this quite stressful. For priests like Phil Foley and Dean Ahern any enterprise no matter how demanding was no more than a challenge towards achievement.

– THE STUDENT IN MAYNOOTH –

From this you can see that, for me, going to Maynooth to prepare for priesthood was a natural progression. I had before me a good model in Fr Phil Foley. I loved life in Maynooth. Little did I realise when I entered in 1949 that I would see out more than thirty years there and that these thirty years would happen to be the most significant in the history of the College. When among one hundred others I entered its gates for the first time, Maynooth, then the largest seminary in the world, was steeped in tradition. It had been established by statute of the Irish Parliament in 1795 for the education of those of the Popish religion as a means of keeping at bay the revolutionary ideas on the Continent. Seminaries there had been for centuries training priests for the Irish mission during the harsh British regime in Ireland. At the centenary in 1895 Maynooth had been given the status of Pontifical University and in 1927 it had been recognised as a college of the National University of Ireland. That was the historical background. In day-to-day life Maynooth had something of a timeless quality about it when over a hundred of us new seminarians gathered there from the four corners of Ireland. The accents from Derry and Belfast were to be a challenge for us as our Cork accent was to be for them.

As we entered between the pair of inscrutable sphinxes that guarded the main gate we must have cut strange awkward figures in our jet black suits and hats. Those hats! Whatever about their usage by older men at that time, they felt and looked ridiculous on us raw youths. We accepted without question that this was standard uniform for clerical students, as it was for Irish priests for many decades afterwards. In fact it was established as *de rigeur* by a statute of the 1956 Maynooth Synod. Bishop John Ahern, who did not feel comfortable in a hat, apart from formal occasions always carried it. Some wag explained that with his legal mind he read the phrase *portat capellam* literally as 'carry a hat' rather than 'wear a hat'.

After the hat it was a small step then to don the black soutane and three-cornered biretta. In hindsight one asks whether the way of life in Maynooth was planned to run on parallel lines to that of military cadets. Whether deliberate or not the same sense of discipline motivated our programme of life. We were all there to be formed in the same mould so as to act in concert under obedience. Any sign of 'singularity' would be suppressed. The uniform was the great leveller on both fronts. I suppose it suited well enough for life in a settled ecclesiastical culture such as that of Ireland in the fifties. There was little store set on individual initiative and no sense of need for training in forms of leadership. 'Ours not to ask the reason why. Ours just to do and die.' That left us ill-prepared for the world that we would meet after ordination. We were formed to maintain a tried and tested system in the church culture of the time. We were to paddle in a lagoon. It would have taken a prophet of extraordinary foresight to forecast the maelstrom that would await us beyond the reef some decades ahead. Evidence of how protected we were from the world outside is now hard to credit. The contemporary newspapers tended to be serious sober reports and analyses of current affairs. College rules banned access to them. Anyone caught with the old crystal set radio faced summary expulsion. Were it not for the Christmas break and the long summer holidays we would have been hermits.

Here were the cream of intellectual Irish youth and yet so few were to achieve their potential in confronting the challenges of the world that awaited them. Clericalism had taken over our personalities to the point of blinding us to its limitations in meeting the pastoral challenges of a new era. One of our teachers, Canon JG McGarry, was an independent figure and a free spirit. His foresight led him in 1950 to establish *The Furrow* as a journal for charting future directions for the Church in Ireland. The journal became a beacon and gained credibility for Maynooth among Irish priests the world over. At that stage his vision seemed idealistic rather than realistic. However, it bore fruit later in inspiring support for the Maynooth Union Summer School which attracted speakers of the quality of Cardinals Josef Ratzinger and Franz Koenig, both of whom had been leading lights at the Second Vatican Council.

Of course, all this is hindsight. As seminarians we settled into life in Maynooth. We had spiritual direction provided by two Vincentian fathers who brought a human quality into what was otherwise a Spartan regime. Under the watchful eye of the Dean, observation of the rules was strict. Some students would be directed to leave as unsuitable for life in the seminary. This was the ultimate sanction. The more immediate censure was exclusion from the list of students approved for the various steps towards ordination.

This list was published orally on a day towards end of term known as Black Friday. It was met with foreboding. Still and all, comparatively few students failed to continue towards priesthood. The bonds forged with those who did leave were not severed by departure. On the whole they remained close to their classmates and loyal to the memory of the College. It is good to see their eyes light up as they meet you and proudly introduce their families. They are still a valued constituency for the College, ready to be called on whenever support is needed by their Alma Mater.

Naturally much of the time in Maynooth, apart from spiritual exercises, was committed to study. First came the three-year NUI accredited course in Philosophy and Arts/Science. We were too inexperienced and immature to appreciate what pure philosophy was all about. It was providing answers to fundamental questions about the meaning of existence. The problem was that we had never asked the questions for ourselves and so the answers had nothing on which to roost. In the absence of a mature enquiring mind philosophical concepts are stillborn on the pages of a book.

To us at the time the subjects in the course on philosophy were presented as cut-and-dried rather than as issues to be explored. It was intended as a preparation for theology to foster the intellectual search and familiarise one with techniques of thinking and analysing. Looking back I feel that only the exercises in logic proved useful in that course on philosophy. Logic sharpened the critical sense in the process of debate and argument and in assessing the validity of conclusions. This and the course on ethics served us particularly well later on as we came to study moral theology. Indeed, the ethics programme centred on themes which would later be studied again in moral theology. Ethics set that agenda. In that first three years leading to the B.A. in addition to philosophy, I followed the course in classical Greek and Latin. An t-Athair Donncha O'Floinn, whose family hailed from Kanturk, was a gifted Irish teacher. He taught us in First Arts and advised that I continue with Celtic Studies. However, Bishop James Roche directed that I take Latin and Greek as preparation for theology. Here we had equally gifted professors in Dr Denis Meehan and Dr John Hackett. The logical structure of language and the clear expression of meaning were valuable assets to understanding classical literature, which was not given to loose thinking or overstatement. As that literature was presented and analysed one came to appreciate why it was called 'classical' and why it has been so basic to western civilisation.

What a pity that those languages were too often taught at Second Level just in terms of grammar and syntax! What a gain it is today that students who enjoy the Classical Civilisation courses at Third Level are inspired to return to learn the actual languages! I have met a young student in a remote part of Kerry who had been so inspired in her course at NUI Galway that she had taken on post-graduate research. Her choice of study was the language which Greek philosophy had contributed to the development of sacramental theology. Well, it made my day!

Latin and Greek operated as key to the study of Christian theology. This certainly would apply to any research into the early sources. It also applied to the standard text books used in the theology syllabus of the time. The professors taught their classes in English but would constantly refer to the Latin textbooks. For those of us familiar with the language this was not too much of a problem. For others it was a major barrier. Rome was committed to preserving the Latin language as *lingua franca* in Pontifical Universities. When John XXIII became Pope one of his first encyclical letters *Veterum Sapientia* (The Wisdom of the Ancients) aimed to promote the use of Latin. It required that for theology degrees in Pontifical Universities professors should teach their classes through Latin. When I came myself to teach theology we made a gesture towards that requirement by providing summaries in Latin. It was a hopeless compromise. To make fun of the effort one student wag translated *caveat emptor* as 'return the empties'.

The final four years of formation in Maynooth passed quickly enough. The camaraderie amongst one's fellow diocesans and classmates shortened the winters. Then there were the sports fields, tennis courts and handball alleys. There was no lack of opportunity for handicrafts. I spent many a happy hour in the carpentry shop making bookcases, garden seats and whatever else presented itself. This combined very well with an interest in beekeeping.

We turned out state-of-the-art beehives for a ready-made apiary in the sunny corner of an old walled garden. It was an ideal location. There we introduced Italian queens from those bred by the famous Brother Adam in Buckfast Abbey in England. There we cut down surplus queen cells to control swarming and housed any swarm that would emerge in spite of our best efforts so as to keep all bees hard at work. I still look back with deep contentment on those glorious summer evenings. This was the Maynooth that was a home from home for many of us.

On the Golden Jubilee of ordination to priesthood celebrated in Maynooth in June 2006 it was gratifying to meet over forty members of our class. Someone said that he had expected to see more sticks than legs! Well there we were, hale and hearty and still committed to working in the Lord's vineyard while we had the health and the strength. There was a poignant moment when the litany of deceased colleagues was read out during our Mass for the Dead. We knew that we were into the eleventh hour and prayed that the Lord would gather us all into his home in heaven. Amen, a Thiarna.

CHAPTER 3

PRIEST AND TEACHER

Ordination to the priesthood in June 1956 was surely a red-letter day. In a long line dressed in white albs we moved in procession up the aisle towards the sanctuary of the great College chapel. There we would prostrate before the altar where Archbishop John Charles McQuaid of Dublin presided. Behind us in the choir stalls were our families and friends gathered from the four corners of Ireland. It was an awesome experience for everyone. I was as tense and serious as the others must have been as I pledged myself with a yes to carry out the vocation of the priesthood with the help of God. We were certain that in committing ourselves we would be supported by the prayers of our families and of the whole community.

Each time I attend an ordination ceremony my memory will take me back to that day in Maynooth half a century ago. Seeing another young priest pledging his yes at the altar acts better than any retreat in terms of the challenge it presents to oneself. Of course, in the numbers that respond to the call to priesthood in Ireland there has been a very serious decline. Where there would have been one hundred candidates per year there is now a fraction of that number. It is a symptom of a major culture shift in both family and society. Offering to serve as a priest today takes independent courage and self-knowledge as well as a profound personal sense of pledging oneself to follow in the footsteps of Jesus no matter what life may bring. Now as never before do those words of the Gospel hold good: 'No one putting his hand to the plough and looking back is fit for the Kingdom.'

Well, when we put hand to plough that June morning in Maynooth we did not feel alone and we were not striking out into the unknown. There was certainly no sense of crisis. We were leaving everything in the hands of God – and of the Bishop. At that time the Diocese of Cloyne had more than sufficient priests for the home mission. Four of my colleagues – Michael Condon, Con O'Donovan, Finbar Kelleher and Vincent O'Donoghue – were temporarily assigned to parishes in England. I already knew that Bishop James Roche had indicated that I should return to Maynooth for further studies in theology. However, he died that summer and I saw this as a reprieve.

Happy as I had been in Maynooth a break for pastoral work would have been welcome. Monsignor James Sheedy of Mallow, who as Vicar Capitular in the *inter-regnum* governed the Diocese, appointed me temporarily to Doneraile. There was a further attraction there in having the Awbeg river close to hand. I had just about settled in at the old presbytery, where Canon Sheehan had once worked at writing his many books, when the new Bishop of Cloyne, Dr John Ahern, himself a Professor of Canon Law in Maynooth, was appointed bishop. One of his first acts was to direct that I return to the College for post-graduate studies in canon law.

– FURTHER STUDIES –

While canon law in Maynooth was excellently taught to seminarians there was no great tradition of its study at post-graduate level. Some of Bishop Ahern's erstwhile colleagues on the theological staff succeeded in bringing him to change his mind. I then really enjoyed the two years working towards the doctorate in theology. I am particularly grateful to my former Professor of Greek, Dr John Hackett. In presence he was shy and retiring but behind that was a very active enquiring mind. It was his recommendation of a topic for research that coloured my future course of study in theology.

For the first time I heard from him about Dom Odo Casel, a Benedictine liturgical scholar gifted with extraordinary insight. One reads a symbolic significance in his death as he collapsed after intoning the *Exsultet* hymn while celebrating the Paschal Mystery at Easter 1949. That Paschal Mystery was the heart of his theology. Dom Odo's particular insight was to link the concepts of Greek mystery–philosophy with the development of the Christian theology of sacrament. Traditionally the Christian Church had looked to Old Testament Judaism for the main source of its sacramental theology, particularly that of the Eucharist. Dom Odo stressed that the most influential early theologians were Greek in mind and language. It was they who have given us the theological concepts through which we understand sacraments. Greek mystery–philosophy in his view was by divine providence the cradle, the *vorschule* as he titled it, of how the Church came to understand and express its faith in sacraments. Did not the early Creeds depend on concepts worked out against a background of Greek philosophy? Why not then the theology of sacraments?

In that address to his academic audience in Regensburg University on 14 September 2006 Pope Benedict XVI took up this same theme under the title 'Faith, Reason and the University: Memories and Reflections'. Unfortunately his whole thesis was sidelined by the brouhaha about a quotation which he had cited from an eastern source six centuries back. Moslems saw it as an insult to their Prophet Muhammed. It was a disappointment that he did not get a hearing for his main thesis on how the interlinking of Scripture and Greek Philosophy had been providential in relating Christian Faith to Human Reason. Dom Odo Casel had already done something similar in his theology of sacrament.

It was certainly an inspiring vision but also a daunting challenge to analyse Dom Odo's teaching. Dr John Hackett offered to be on call for direction as needed when members of staff in theology said that the subject was not practicable. One man said that a doctorate dissertation should aim to be a raft to get you across the stream to the other bank, not a boat to launch out on a current to God-knows-where! Of course he was right. I had to trim sail to a specific focus. That focus was the understanding by St Paul in his Letter to the Romans, chapter 6, on Christian Baptism as symbolising Death and Resurrection with Christ.

Even with that focus I was still struggling against a headwind. Dom Odo Casel had certainly written plenty and had been driven to clarify his ideas in response to various controversies. If he had written one decent book one would have a solid anchor against being driven hopelessly around the course. Getting at the original sources required then an inter-library trawl, unlike today with its websites and search engines. Still, librarians all over Europe could not have been more helpful, particularly those with Benedictine associations. I had acquired a fair reading knowledge of French and Italian but German, in which Dom Odo had mainly written, was more difficult. It didn't even read like a modern language with all those complicated portmanteau terms.

Maynooth had a fine theological library of standard Latin texts, ancient and modern. There was little enough in contemporary European theology. One of those contemporary writers who was pushing out the boat alongside Dom Odo Casel was Edouard Schillebeeckx, a Dutch Dominican. Even though he never did get around to completing his major enterprise on sacramental theology in the footsteps of the *Summa Theologica* of Thomas Aquinas, he had published an introductory volume *Christ, the Sacrament of God*. When Dom Odo's insights would later have a major influence on the Liturgy Constitution of the Second Vatican Council it would have been chiefly Schillebeeckx who had mediated them. Anyway for me, with a comprehensive body of Greek and Latin source material at hand in Maynooth, I was in a position to analyse Dom Odo's understanding of the mystery of Christian Baptism against its background in Greek tradition. It was a fascinating enquiry.

At the end of the two years the dissertation was submitted to the Faculty of Theology. The appointed readers were Professors Patrick Corish and Jeremiah Newman. A doctoral examination in Maynooth at that time was a stressful if not indeed a shattering experience. It was little consolation to know that the very first doctorate degree awarded in Maynooth after its accreditation as Pontifical University in 1795 had left the candidate mentally unbalanced! By coincidence the priest in question was a Fr Dineen of the Diocese of Cloyne! The intervening century and a half had somewhat familiarised candidates with the system. It was still an ordeal for the few of us who advanced to qualification.

The examining panel numbered all members of the Faculty of Theology with the addition of one extern examiner. It amounted to a two-hour session. The first half hour comprised a model lecture in Latin on a theme given to the candidate on the previous evening by the Dean of the Faculty. Then the extern would select a proposition from a list of fifty submitted by the candidate and he would argue the case as a kind of *advocatus diaboli*. That left an hour for the 'defence' of the dissertation against the reservations of the two appointed readers. I was fortunate in having two readers who had done their homework well and who set a lively tone to the debate. Even so, it was literally a baptism of fire. One could see how that first initiate ended up a broken man! Some years later in Rome I saw how matter-of-course these examinations tended to be there. In Maynooth they have also become more humane.

– ROME AND THE VATICAN COUNCIL –

In the course of that summer of 1958, Bishop John Ahern directed me to submit an application for one of the two advertised posts in Theology and Canon Law in Maynooth.

Enda McDonagh and I were appointed to teach moral theology with the proviso that we would further qualify in canon law to bring that faculty up to strength. Enda went to Rome and Munich to attain the necessary qualification while I fell in teaching moral theology in Maynooth. During those two years I stayed with the standard textbook in class but read widely as well. It is said that in one's first year teaching one teaches more than one knows oneself, in the second year one teaches more than students need to know and in the third year one teaches what students require to know!

When Enda returned with his canon law doctorate in 1960 I went out to qualify similarly. It was an exciting time in Rome, on the very eve of the Second Vatican Council. The massive undertaking had struck the Church like a bombshell, all due to the inspiration of the elderly Pope John XXIII. The story goes that when he shared his conviction with his secretary the startled priest had glanced at him quizzically and remarked that he might be too old to take on a task of this nature.

Anyway, as I arrived in the Collegio Irlandese on Via dei SS. Quattro preparations for an Ecumenical Council were in train. Already there had been a palace revolution when representatives of the European bishops had judged unacceptable the draft documents prepared by Curia executives at the Vatican. The bishops required a more thoroughgoing pastoral approach which would deal with prevailing challenges to preaching the Gospel.

What a time to be in Rome! Theologians whom one had read – or just read about! – were now to be seen and heard. Rahner, Ratzinger, Schillebeeckx, Delhaye, De Lubac, Danielou, Congar, Philips, Häring. Here were names to conjure with wherever scholarly groups got together. These were among the key advisers to the bishops and it was they who burned the midnight oil in putting together the alternative drafts requested by the bishops to guide the deliberations at the Council.

There were sideshows of which we were keen observers. One such sideshow was the controversy between two schools of scriptural studies represented by the Biblicum and the Lateran University. For the Lateran, where traditionalists had correctly realised that Scripture would be of central importance in the Council, the campaign was launched as a pre-emptive strike against the latter day 'Modernists'. The key questions turned on Biblical Hermeneutic on how to interpret the Bible. The Biblicum, attached to the Gregorian University and closely allied with the École Biblique in Jerusalem, rolled out a vast specialist cohort to which the opposition did not have an answer. The controversy waxed hot and heavy with more heat than light until it was reported that behind the scenes Pope John XXIII intervened to bring closure. Unfortunately, my file of broadsheets built up from those distributed by student supporters on both sides has been lost – or rather not returned by a colleague who had 'borrowed' it. It would still make for good reading. One wag circulated a joke on Cardinal Ottaviani hailing a taxi across to the Council. Deep in his documents he did not notice that he was well into the countryside. *Dov'andiamo?* He asked the driver. *Al Concilio, padre, si. Al Concilio di Trento!* (relating back five centuries to the Council of Trent!) Ottaviani was recognised as leader of the conservative wing.

Amid all this excitement I continued with more serious study, chiefly in Moral Theology. Here I had two outstanding mentors in Josef Fuchs in the Gregorian University and Bernard Häring in the Alphonsianum. I have had occasion already to write about how much they left me in their debt. Both saw that Moral Theology should take inspiration from Scripture and not only direction from a code of law – and that Canon Law itself should be inspired from that same source. I wished then that I could be spending time in Rome in the study of Scripture rather than of Canon Law.

Two themes in particular have been treasured by me from conferences with those masters in moral and pastoral theology.

The themes took their inspiration directly from the teaching of Jesus in the Gospel. Later on I saw that approach endorsed by the Vatican Council in its *Decree on Priestly Formation*:

> Special attention needs to be given to the development of moral theology. Its scientific exposition should be more thoroughly nourished by the teaching of Scripture. It should show the nobility of the Christian vocation of the faithful, and their obligation to bring forth fruit in charity for the life of the world. (par. 16)

The first of those themes is the balance between the Witness to Truth and the Witness to Compassion. The former stresses the challenge of living up to the imperatives of moral truth. This moral truth is a datum, a given reality which conscience must search out and respect as having meaning in itself. The latter introduces the concept of pastoral understanding for the human situation where personal circumstances always have an influence. This concept is well expressed in the Greek term *synkatabasis*, literally 'condescension'. Putting forward the Witness to Truth without thought for the Witness to Compassion leads to moral authoritarianism whereas taking the opposite course leads to moral anarchy. Both witnesses should run in tandem.

We see how Jesus preserves that fine balance in his manner of dealing with the situation of the adulterous woman in chapter 8 of the Gospel of John. The Scribes and Pharisees had baited a trap for him by presenting the woman for his verdict. It is a dramatic scene, the original Catch-22 situation. He neatly turns the tables on them and when they have left in disarray he addresses the woman: 'Has no one condemned you? ... Neither do I condemn you; go, and do not sin again.'

The second theme was then a matter of current interest in Rome. It was that of the Existential Ethic which had been recently brought into focus by Karl Rahner. In a way I think that he was concerned that the strong official condemnation of Situation Ethics at that time may have led to overkill on the other side. In rough terms the criticised Situation Ethics saw the individual situation as the determinant of moral obligation for the person. This led to permissiveness and licence. The resultant stress by Church authority on the binding force of objective universal norms left the imperative of the individual call out of the equation.

This Existential Ethic in Rahner's understanding amounts to a concrete moral demand on the individual in his particular circumstance. Christian morality should not then be presented simply as a morality of general rules and directives. Christian conscience is called on to discern the will of God over and above these in terms of the talents, graces and opportunities which are placed in one's way. To quote Rahner himself: 'Norms are universal, but man as an existent is individual and unique in each case, and hence he cannot be regulated in his actions only by material norms of a universal kind.' This brings into play how St Thomas Aquinas defined the virtue of prudence as positive decision making rather than just pastoral caution.

It is evident that here we have a clear reflection of what Jesus taught in the Gospel. The Parable of the Talents is a good model of the Existential Ethic. 'To whom more is granted from him more is expected.' In other words the individual *will* be called to meet the universal norm in his or her particular way and *may* be called on to go beyond what it generally requires. Look at Zacchaeus shinning down that sycamore tree, committing himself to paying over the odds in restitution!

It is not a comfortable ethic. One cannot take pride in judging oneself better than others. We simply do not know the limitations that they experience. As the proverb of the native Indians in America expressed it, you never know what a man's life is until you have walked a day in his moccasins. About ourselves we should agree with Scripture: 'We are unprofitable servants. We have done no more than what we were required to do.' So Rahner asks: 'Could not an Existential Ethic help us to see more clearly that sin, over and above its property of being an offence against the law of God, is also and just as much an offence against an utterly individual imperative of the individual will of God, which is the basis of uniqueness?'

However, my two years in Rome were running on and qualification in canon law was pressing. When one comes to appreciate what Rome has to offer in resources for study in the field of canon law one realises how far Maynooth falls short in access to the sources. The Dean of the Faculty of Canon Law in the Lateran University was a very fair-minded man. He was a Conventual Franciscan, Pietro Tocanel, of a definite pastoral turn of mind. One frequently saw him in the confessional at the Lateran Basilica. He taught me a good deal about how Rome assessed the human condition. 'Un po' di úmanità!' It was not quite the satirical story of the two sets of bronze angels on the Pont de San Angelo. One pair points to the Vatican with 'That is where the law is made'; the other points outwards: 'That is where it is kept'. He generously allowed me credits for the main courses which I had studied and taught in Maynooth. That left me with the more marginal, and indeed with the more interesting, areas in the syllabus.

Already on arrival at Rome I had identified a theme for a future dissertation, a theme which ran in tandem with ethics. It was the principle that a law made to guard against a general risk binds even in individual cases where the risk itself does not apply. What intrigued me was that the relevant principle cited in the Code of Canon Law at can. 21 did not have the typical standard reference to sources or *fontes*. These *fontes* were glosses on the individual canons indicating the background legal context. Cardinal Pietro Gasparri, the scholarly compiler of the 1918 Code of Canon Law and its five volumes of *fontes*, did not indicate any sources in terms of earlier authorities for can. 21. Hence the question: 'Where did this particular principle in canon law come from?'

It was not just an academic enquiry. The principle still applies for very practical issues. If one is prosecuted for driving while exceeding the established alcohol limit it is not a good defence to claim that the amount actually leaves you personally as sober as the judge. Before 1600, if you pardon the anachronism, that would have passed as a fair defence because the law would have been read as based on a presumption which the evidence in the individual case could rebut. Around 1600, three influential Jesuit canonists, Suarez, Vasquez and De Salas, questioned the justification for the use of presumption in this context. They concluded that the law was focused not on a presumption of fact but on a well-founded conviction of a general risk. It was this which later motivated the legislators to establish the prohibition across the board.

The reasoning might not qualify as breaking the Da Vinci Code but it was an interesting hunt for a solution to the what and the why. It carried me back to make the acquaintance of the gifted *magistri legis* who had authoritatively established the force of the Roman civil law as codified by the emperor Justinian. Their views have influenced European law and canon law for fifteen centuries. One appreciates that the change of principle in 1600 strengthened the hand of the law in curbing individual liberty – or licence, if you wish. I was fortunate in having so interesting a theme for a dissertation. Most doctorate dissertations in canon law tend to be dry and uninspiring with little reference to real life, or to any imaginative search for background. I was fortunate in researching a colourful point in philosophy of law. Why, for instance, did the book of a Roman Cardinal challenging that change of principle in the seventeenth century disappear from libraries without any evidence of suppression? Was it quietly killed off when it was seen as outmoded by the new consensus?

I certainly enjoyed my two years in Rome in every respect. Maynooth accepted my stay as a quasi-sabbatical and allowed me my salary, then the princely sum of £320 *per annum*. That went to fund trips with fellow students to Sicily, Capri, Ischia or wherever. But, then, why leave Rome at all? The Collegio Irlandese was at the heart of ancient Rome, a stone's throw from where Julius Caesar had entered the Forum in triumph and where Nero had organised gladiatorial shows for the populace. Then everywhere you turned there were memories taking one back to the cradle of Christianity where Peter and Paul and innumerable martyrs had died for the Christian faith. During my time there the excavations under the crypt of St Peter's Basilica had revealed what, on all the evidence, are accepted as the bones of Peter himself. If that site is not suffused with a *genius loci,* what site is?

It was a very full two years. The Collegio Irlandese was a happy place with constant welcome for guests passing through Rome. There the various Irish festivals were celebrated with traditional hospitality. It was there I made the acquaintance of the forbidding figure of the Benedictine Dom Peter Flood: philosopher, obstetrician, monk, in that order. I never did get the full story of his series of qualifications, funded, I think, by some trust established by his deceased parents. In the operating theatre he had been the terror of nurses who did not read his mind as he barked commands. As he cast eyes on me he said: 'The very man! I want you down in the Vicariate to assist in clearing candidates for faculties as confessors.' One did not refuse a request from Dom Peter. Part of his interest was to have someone on hand when a candidate asked to be assessed in Irish!

I cannot leave Rome without a word about our pastoral experience in the local parish. It was organised for two of us Cloyne priests, Martin O'Riordan and myself, by the College Spiritual Director Monsignor Dominic Conway, later Bishop of Elphin. The parish priest of the neighbouring Navicella parish was the gentle Don Mario. I never learned his surname even though I have met him since. His directions were simple. Just do what you would do in pastoral work in Ireland. Little did we realise how different the pastoral scene was in Italy. We discovered that while religious practice was confined to the major feasts of the Christian year there was a deep sense of spirituality in personal and family life. A query about Sunday Mass might attract the response *Sono catolico, ma non fanatico*! (A Catholic but not a fanatic!) An important milestone was the blessing of homes at Easter. Apart from this we would visit apartments blocks as the caretaker, the portiera, would direct us. The idea of Italian priests visiting homes would not have been contemplated.

It was on one such visit that I came to meet Senora Lanza. She explained that the photograph on her windowsill was of her son, who had been teaching moral theology in Rome. I told her that I had the Lanza-Palazzini series of textbooks published jointly by him and a colleague in the Lateran University. She said that her son had been appointed bishop in Rhegio-Calabria in the south of Italy. In setting out to impose discipline on the diocese she claimed that he had been murdered by the Mafia in collusion with some priests. On checking back with the Rector, Monsignor Donal Herlihy, he admitted that there had been a mystery about Archbishop Lanza's death. This was a sobering insight into the dark side of Church life in southern Italy.

Finally, on a lighter note, I recall a pastoral experience that Martin O'Riordan and I had on the island of Ischia in the Bay of Naples. It was Easter and we offered to assist the local parish priest. On Holy Thursday we were ready in the confessionals. Penitents were sparse at first but then numbers began to arrive. We learned that word had gone out that there were two American chaplains without any knowledge of Ischone, the local dialect! It became what we at home would call a 'field day': open to all comers. I had been too ready to accept that the term *bugia* in all Italian dialects would translate simply as the word for lie. One lives and learns.

– RETURN TO MAYNOOTH –

After that 1960–1962 sojourn in Rome Maynooth was a calm haven where life continued as heretofore. But not for long. On 11 October 1962 the Second Vatican Council formally opened. Its first act was to promulgate a Message to Humanity. This had been drafted by a group of French bishops and theologians with the approval of Pope John XXIII. It was a most inspiring statement on the themes and issues which the Council would be addressing. It should be studied by anyone who wishes to identify the 'spirit of Vatican II', a much abused phrase in subsequent years. That spirit is explained there as rooted in the message of the Gospel and in listening to what the Holy Spirit was saying in and to the Church.

It should not have come as a surprise that the Message to Humanity had been inspired and drafted by a group representing the Church in France. Where Germany exerted a strong influence on specialist academic theology, France had built on a positive tradition of pastoral theology, dealing with living the Gospel rather than analysing theological concepts. We in Ireland should have learned more from that French tradition. We would then have had a better appreciation of the issues on which the Pastoral Council came to focus attention. As it was we were given answers to questions which we had not even asked, even though we prided ourselves on our pastoral gifts.

Of course with hindsight we can plead in defence that the religious culture in France, refined in the crucible of secular liberalism after the French Revolution, was totally different from that in Ireland where Church and State side-by-side had provided us with our national identity. There was little sense of a need for forward thinking. Tradition held firm. When Archbishop John Charles McQuaid returned after his first sojourn in Rome at the Council he assured his people in so many words that nothing would disturb the tranquillity of their Christian lives. The Council might just be a hiccup.

That comment reflected the mindset of many Irish priests and bishops at the time. In a word, the Council caught us unready. If we had been so prepared, what a role we would have played in guiding bishops of the Irish diaspora during the deliberations at the Council! Those bishops with their great respect for their Irish Catholic background looked to us for that leadership.

Those of us in Maynooth who had studied outside the country had less excuse to lie low or, as one wag said, to continue to ply sleeping dogs with tranquillisers. There was pressure to get our teaching of theology up to speed with the Council. In the absence of up-to-date textbooks it was very much hit-and-miss. We could and should have done a great deal more for our students if we had showed more foresight and courage.

Later Maynooth experienced the back-wash from the student turmoil which had convulsed Europe in 1968. Our students confronted us teachers with a critique of the programme of studies in theology classes. While some of the proposals were superficial others were truly substantial. Of these we then took notice but I feel that long before as a faculty we should have given more time to planning and to launching out into the deep as a new future beckoned. In a way we were standing on two boats with a foot in each. It is not a comfortable position. We were stitching the themes and insights of the Council on to the traditional textbook pattern. Putting new wine into old bottles. Of course, it is easy to be wise after the event. We certainly were on a learning curve but we should have shortened the trajectory.

During that process of questioning the standard theology programme, the students chose a first-class mentor in Professor Peter Connolly of the Department of English. It was an inspired choice. He was one of the most independent critical minds in Maynooth and had the total confidence of the students. He winnowed the wheat from the chaff and explained how any true 'pastoral theology' would require the study of deep theological matters as well as training on practical pastoral issues. Peter Connolly's sheaf of articles in *The Furrow* of the time still crackle with their sense of immediacy. Where cant and sloppy thinking came the way he did not take prisoners. His weapon was the rapier rather than the broadsword. He was not appreciated by the powers-that-be at the time. They took particular exception to an article in the *Irish Theological Quarterly* which included actual quotations to indicate the contrast between straight pornography and genuine literature.

In the Maynooth Union Summer School we already had a vehicle where priests and lay people could gather to discuss current issues in theology. This provided an opportunity to invite speakers from abroad. That mention of lay people is relevant. A major impact of the Council here was seen in the growth of a strong interest in theology among educated lay people. In contrast to Britain we did not have an articulate laity ready to intervene publicly on issues of Christian belief and practice. This was seen in Ireland as the province of the clergy and indeed still is to a large extent.

As the Council got under way the Dominican Fr Austin Flannery gathered a group of interested lay people including journalists, the late Sean MacReamonn and John Horgan. At that time little hard information was provided by official sources in Rome about the deliberations on the floor of the Council. It now seems unbelievable that an event of that importance for Christians worldwide should have been conducted behind closed doors. By the second session the secrecy was considerably relaxed because so much had been coming out through unofficial sources with a slant to the sensational. Anyway, Fr Flannery's group had quite good contacts in Rome. Discussion would have been well informed and lively. At the time it would have been good to have some bishops join in and add more substance to the debate. Bishops then kept their distance from this form of exposure. Perhaps they were right. It was a pretty irreverent gathering of independent minds. They first met in a pub in Dún Laoghaire. They were known as the Plaster Saints. When they earned the soubriquet Plastered Saints they moved into more sober premises in Dublin!

After the Council many well-qualified men and women were invited to become members of the many Church Commissions then established. Some of these Commissions remained little more than a listing of members' names in the annual *Irish Catholic Directory*. In the absence of a specific agenda they were more sinecures than working groups. One glorious exception was the Catholic Marriage Advisory Council (CMAC). This was developed first in Britain under the leadership of an inspired priest of Westminster Archdiocese, Canon Maurice O'Leary. Even though not a native son of Ireland he loved everything about the Irish. In a short time he extended CMAC to Ireland as well, aggregating some of us in Maynooth as a kind of think tank.

Here was the oxygen to power pastoral thinking. The great majority of those associated with CMAC were professionals: many trained in counselling skills and a good sprinkling of doctors. They took nothing for granted and honestly confronted any issues that came the way. It was a pleasure to be exchanging views with a group of that quality. I found it informing and stimulating. Even when Ireland set up its own marriage counselling system, now known as ACCORD, Canon O'Leary was always looked on as founding father and attended annual conferences until his death.

The link with CMAC had provided an outreach to a mainly lay professional group. It had a formative influence on me in providing an opportunity to appreciate the competence of lay people in Church ministry. Here were people of deep faith and of strong commitment ready to instil true human and Christian values into family life, the area in which they were experts. It was my first hands-on experience of lay ministry in action. I was also impressed by the CMAC priests who saw themselves as collaborators in a joint task. The mutual respect and

Christian spirit so evident in CMAC spelled for me the eventual death of clericalism.

There seems to be some congenital leaning towards clericalism in us Irish priests. It affects not just those on the home mission but very many of those in the diaspora as well. Working with CMAC provided an effective antidote, for me at any rate. Up to that we priests would have called in qualified lay people for direction on specific issues within their competence. In a way it was buying in lay expertise but not really involving lay people in managing and planning, in deciding policy and implementing decisions as members of a team. This is where CMAC was different. Here were professional lay people not just providing a service but actually committing themselves to Christian ministry side-by-side with priests. It was a God-given grace to share that experience. It has made me impatient with the clerical psyche and a mindset which so distorts appreciation of what the Church should be.

– THE *HUMANAE VITAE* CONTROVERSY –

The publication in 1968 of Pope Paul VI's encyclical letter *Humanae vitae* was a challenge for CMAC. Under the guidance of Canon O'Leary the practical policy was confirmed that CMAC would continue to provide advice and direction in keeping with the now reaffirmed teaching of the Catholic Church. This avoided friction between members who would continue to hold personal views on the rights and wrongs of that teaching. CMAC was convinced of the values for family life which commitment to the use of the infertile period reflected and promoted. It should represent an attitude of recognition for the role of God in bringing new life into being and a generous welcome for that new life under God as Creator. It should inspire that level of mutual understanding between husband and wife which collaboration in the use of the method required. In a word, CMAC focused on the pastoral value rather than on the intrinsic logic of the teaching on birth control.

In popular parlance at the time any mention of the infertile period as a means of spacing and limiting births would have been dismissed as advocating a form of Vatican Roulette. The CMAC was convinced through its own experiences with numerous clients and through the work of its specialist members that the principle was soundly based. A great deal of time and energy was invested in perfecting and promoting it. One person stands out in that record: Dr John Marshall of London.

The credibility of the use of the infertile period had been compromised by the outmoded calendar method of identifying it. The principle was quite correct but the use of this particular method led to relatively poor results. It was here that CMAC research, in conjunction with that of others, made a breakthrough by identifying the slight rise in temperature at the time of ovulation. This advanced to become the sympto-thermal method which is now in widespread use. When a couple act in collaboration with a common purpose this method compares well in accuracy with that of the contraceptive pill. In terms of user attitude it is more acceptable because it does not imply any invasive medication. In today's culture of natural treatments it also gains from that association.

CMAC did not envisage nor did it promote the use of the infertile period as the Catholic answer to contraception. Its policy was far more positive. It promoted it as a way of deepening a couple's love and respect for one another through building up an emotional rapport beyond that of the physical sex experience. For Christians there was the overall sense of God as Creator engaged in the mystery of bringing new life into being. In a reference to the inherent value of the use of the infertile period, Pope John Paul II occasioned some surprise with a passing comment about the risk of a selfish 'contraceptive' purpose such as the use of the method.

While the crisis was well managed by CMAC within its formal remit the general reaction to the encyclical was one of confusion in terms of both theological principle and pastoral practice. At the level of principle there was question as to how the biological pattern of the sexual function could translate into a moral imperative. Was this what logic calls a category error? If one premise in a proposition assumes something which has not been proved the conclusion is questionable on that account. One may still achieve consistency in the desired result but consistency is not substantial truth!

At the level of pastoral practice there was the question of how to deal with situations in family life where there was a serious clash of values. Early reactions were emotional and communicated more heat than light to the debate. Had we fallen into the trap of the Pharisees, tithing out mint and cumin? Precise technological adaptations of the infertile period have led to literal distinctions rather than ethical differences. The AIDS crisis has concentrated minds on physical measures of protection such as the widespread use of condoms. What is now clear is that the promiscuity which this encourages increases the risk of AIDS.

In hindsight one accepts that Pope Paul VI was rightly concerned about the need to shore up the unravelling sexual ethic. He nailed down the principle of respect for the natural sexual function as a barrier against that unravelling. It was more a measure of pastoral concern than of cold logic. Looking back over a generation of embarrassed silence among theologians and bishops one concludes that any ethical principle should have been based on the meaning of human sexuality and on the values which it should reflect rather than on the biological structures of the sexual function. Pope Paul VI did indeed stress those values as the basis of any ethic but the headlines on contraception snuffed out that area of discussion.

Examining the statements on the encyclical issued at the time by hierarchies worldwide one noted a broad spectrum of approaches. The most satisfactory was that of the French bishops in keeping with their pastoral tradition. It expressed an appreciation of how conscience would assess the application of the principle from different viewpoints. It then invoked well-accepted pastoral guidelines for dealing with complex situations.

In a nutshell, when it came to assessing moral accountability, one needed to balance acceptance of the ethical principle with the understanding of a pastoral situation. I found the French approach helpful when invited in 1970 by the Medical Union to sit on a panel to address issues which concerned doctors in practice. The title of the conference was 'Family Planning – the Doctors' Dilemma'. I realised how sensitive this would be in the Archdiocese of Dublin. I looked to my bishop John Ahern for advice. He certainly recognised the dilemma but accepted that I had but one choice. I should go. To decline the invitation offered by such a body would not be an option in terms of credibility for a Maynooth professor. The Archbishop's reaction to my contribution was negative as predicted. I had offered to meet with him in the midst of the media reports but this did not prove possible.

For a general overview of the *Humanae vitae* controversy in Ireland and my predicament and that of others one should read Louise Fuller's *Irish Catholicism since 1950: The Undoing of a Culture*, published by Gill & Macmillan in 2002. This is an outstanding study of the Irish Church in those crucial decades. When history comes to be written *Humanae vitae* will be seen as a watershed in terms of Church authority in Ireland. Everyone could accept that there was an actual physical distinction between methods of birth regulation. The question was whether this constituted an intrinsic moral difference on which to ground the principle. Invoking tradition and authority to substitute for ethical argument put authority itself under question. This opened the door to analysing the role of conscience in arriving at personal decisions about what to do. Once conscience found open space here it could lead to accepting what each one judged right for oneself. In view of the emphasis placed on law and authority in traditional moral theology the concept of one's accountability in conscience had not been sufficiently developed. What now confronted us was the need to substantiate the crucial link between freedom of action and one's responsibility to observe what was true and right. The Council had presented a well-balanced teaching on this very issue. Liberal culture had moved ahead to see truth in the relative terms of what is true for me. The Council's actual teaching would have been the most effective answer to this but the issue of birth control had been specifically withdrawn from the Council's agenda. In the event an appeal to the 'spirit of the Council' was now consciously or unconsciously invoked on the side of individual licence to decide for oneself what affected one's personal life. This groundswell proved intractable. It is essential to find the true balance, else permissiveness rules. The end result is physical coupling in what is called 'recreational sex' based on transient pleasure rather than experiencing the true meaning of human sexuality. Romance and courtship as growth factors in a true relationship are early casualties.

– BROADENING THE PERSPECTIVE –

As the Council was drawing to a close a group from the Faculty of Theology in Maynooth responded to invitations from various Irish dioceses to provide conferences for priests. The group consisted of Kevin McNamara, Enda McDonagh, Donal Flanagan and me. I suppose today we would be known as the Gang of Four. Then we were called the Theological Circus. It was a very worthwhile exercise on our part. First, we had to identify the central issues in the Council documents and develop those in a consistent manner for presentation to priests. Second, we had to learn from exchanges with the priests what issues were important for them.

In the process one was called on to absorb the teaching of the Council and to link this into the pattern of theological thinking with which the audience was familiar. Whereas some earlier analyses of Council teaching stressed, rightly or wrongly, areas of discontinuity we were set to show the continuity with the additional new emphases. It did lead to heated debate at times. I recall an occasion in Glasgow where a priest at one conference stated that he would continue to listen purely as a Roman Catholic observer! The man addressing the audience was Kevin McNamara, who later as Archbishop of Dublin was seen as a thorough traditionalist in theology. One can see how rough the going was when emotions ran high.

Undoubtedly priests were interested. Very many were readers of *The Furrow* and *The Tablet*. Those tended to lead in the exchanges. Naturally the majority would be coming from a solid basis in the traditional theology learned in seminary days. This would have set great store by exact definition. Many of the concepts employed in the Council documents were simply not amenable to exact definition. This was where Vatican I differed from Vatican II in style and direction. The style and direction of Vatican II was inspiring and pastoral. One might say prophetic rather than dogmatic. Concepts did not admit of a logical progression from premises to conclusion. Later on a similar difficulty in deciphering the line of argument would arise in regard to the writings of Pope John Paul II. He thought in the round rather than in straight lines.

This exchange with the priests in the parishes was help to me in the series of pastoral columns which I wrote for *The Furrow* through those years. Formerly I had provided a series on more theological issues in *The Irish Ecclesiastical Record* until it ceased publication in 1969. Comparing both series one sees how there is more of a sense of relevance and reality about that series in *The Furrow*. As time went on personal queries from priests came to swell the volume of the daily post. Unquestionably these queries were a stimulus to research in areas which otherwise would have remained marginal to one's interest. Dealing with this variety of questions was never a chore or a bore. It kept one's feet on the ground and sharpened one's mind.

Another academic area in which I was engaged was in teaching the Medical Ethics course in UCD. This was a major challenge. With medical students in final year you take nothing for granted. Information on the medical front was their strong suit and you deferred to them on that '*is*' factor. Ethics dealt with the '*ought*' factor, the difference between what one can or cannot do and what one ought or ought not do. Evidently this area was ready-made for debate. After all, you cannot dispute established facts, whereas ethical norms are fair game for dispute with a critical audience. On many occasions some area of the debate would spill over into a night session at one or other of the university societies.

In bridging the '*is*' and the '*ought*' I once used a parable to distinguish between cold intellect and basic commonsense. The personnel in a plane are Richard Nixon, President of the United States, Henry Kissinger, Secretary of State, a bishop and a hippie. The plane is about to ditch and the pilot directs that they don parachutes and bail out. They discover just three parachutes. Nixon claims priority as key man in the balance of world power. Kissinger stresses that some crucial peace negotiations depend on his intellect. When both have gone the bishop urges the hippie to take the remaining parachute and leave with his blessing. The hippie responds: 'No sweat, bishop, the man with all that intellect has gone off with my rucksack.' No doubt when the content of the course was long forgotten by the class the memory of the story remained. Ethics is just enlightened commonsense.

One gathers that university life now has become so focused on qualifying for one's degree that college societies barely survive for lack of audience. What a shame. University life used to be all about stretching the mind and not just absorbing information. Certainly a programme in medical ethics gave space for stretching the mind. One can imagine how medical students faced with so much factual information found the course in ethics a relief and a release. They certainly pitched in and used the chance for wide-ranging debate.

How did the lecturer survive and teach a course? In a word, by being honest and up-front. I made no apology for the fact that I was a Catholic priest. I wore the collar with the academic gown. The great majority of students were Catholics with some other Christians and a few Moslems. I explained that in practice in Ireland most of their patients would be Catholic and so doctors needed to be familiar with that ethical tradition. Where that was at variance with other traditions this would be explained as best I could. The ethical guidelines of the Irish Medical Council were accepted as normative in Ireland. Did I enjoy the experience? Certainly. I lived to tell the tale after those lively sessions in an arena where no quarter was given.

The give-and-take of student interchange in UCD was an indication of a general change in academic culture. Maynooth itself was no longer what it had been when I was first appointed there in 1958. Those might qualify as halcyon days before the maelstrom of the debates around the Second Vatican Council and the protest marches of the Student Movement of the 1960s. The system reflected a tradition which had been consolidated through settled Victorian times. One wag remarked that college life had been organised to serve the convenience of professors rather than the education of students.

Given the amount of development called for on all fronts in the Irish ecclesiastical scene, we in Maynooth who had gained experience in creating structures to meet the current and future needs of the College would have been consulted about similar challenges elsewhere. It was in this fashion that I found myself with a role in St Angela's College of Education for Home Economics on Lough Gill in Sligo. What a glorious location it was as an educational centre, overlooking the lake isle of Innisfree celebrated by WB Yeats. It was in the late seventies that some members of the Ursuline Order visited me in

Maynooth with a request that I advise on establishing academic and governing structures for St Angela's College. They suggested that I give it a weekend. That weekend stretched to more than a decade after basic structures were put in place.

Since its opening in 1952 St Angela's as the flagship of the Ursuline educational system in Ireland had been managed as a family enterprise. Teaching and administrative staff operated on that collaborative basis. In 1978 the College became a recognised College of the National University of Ireland linked to UCG. A structure for management and a system for staff relations were needed. Otherwise the inevitable tensions would have proved difficult to negotiate in what had been a family atmosphere.

A Board of Governors was established with membership drawn from professional bodies on a broad front. What they shared was not just relevant experience but genuine admiration for the work of the Ursuline Order in the development of St Angela's College. Some members had hands-on experience at the highest level in the area of management/staff negotiations. This proved invaluable in the initial period. On their advice the Sisters joined the TUI along with the lay staff so that there would be a common forum. It is to the credit of the TUI that, in contrast to the ASTI, it extended membership to clerics and religious.

I was privileged to serve as chair of the Board of Governors. I learned a great deal in the process, something that really helped when I came to preside later in the County Cork Vocational Education Committee. In that world one came to appreciate the value of teamwork and to recognise the talents of lay professionals. While they appreciated my experience in organising structures for faculties and departments, I certainly appreciated their wisdom in achieving consensus through bringing their expertise to bear on complex human situations. Furthermore, they had close contacts with many national and local politicians. At a time when third level education was in the melting pot this secured a positive hearing for the interests of St Angela's College.

Anyone who came to know St Angela's could not but be impressed. As one dropped down to where it nestled on the shores of Lough Gill one felt one's heart rise. There was an age-old tranquillity about the site where the buildings meshed into the wooded background. There was a welcoming atmosphere even before any friendly greeting was extended to the visitor. The Ursuline Order had spared nothing in adding human quality to what nature had provided as a centre of learning. The threat of rationalisation had cast a shadow over the College for much of my time on the Board of Governors. At first sight its distance from the major centres of population might seem to constitute a problem. As against this it had the potential to provide third level education across the northwest. Over the years this has been the policy which has continued to win the day for St Angela's. Its continued expansion proves the case. The award of an honorary Doctor of Laws on Sr Marianne O'Connor in 2006 was well merited as recognition of her sterling work as President in developing the college over a quarter of a century.

– THE EXPANSION OF MAYNOOTH –

At a time when there was development in all areas of education nationwide, the pace of expansion in Maynooth was frenetic. What had been a major centre for training of priests was now to become a university open to increasing numbers of lay students. If I were to identify when there was most call on time due to college business it was the years when I was both Dean of the Faculty of Theology and Vice-President of the College. During that time the building of the new John Paul II Library was also underway. I was one of a team dealing with planning and funding along with Monsignor Michael Olden, President, and Professor Brendan Devlin, my fellow Vice-President.

The traditional Russell College Library was and is a beautiful building which could compare with any university library in the country. More space was now needed for the increased student numbers. It was also necessary to control the environment for storage of manuscripts, *incunabula* and valuable book collections. A new library for day-to-day student use was required. This was a challenge at a time when other universities were also planning to build similar libraries. The pride of Maynooth was at stake.

The site chosen was the Long Meadow bisected by the Lyrene stream. It could not have been better selected as a location. The design should develop that potential and be worthy of its superb open aspect. The plan was to sequester all library services in a central hub from which the book shelves would radiate, leaving the outside circle available for study and reading in carrels overlooking the Long Meadow. It was an inspired design. The land was gifted by the Trustees. The funds to put the library in place called for an approach to the goodwill of the Maynooth constituency at home and abroad.

What made the early stages of the work with which I was involved so worthwhile was the generosity of those many business people who provided their personal resources and their expertise. It was also valuable experience on how to get decisions promptly taken and effectively implemented. It was a study in time-and-motion. The result is there to be admired as a fine addition to the College.

The library, later christened the John Paul II Library to mark the Pope's visit to Maynooth in 1979, was the culmination of a major process of expansion of the College. This began when Cardinal William Conway became Chairman of the Trustees. It was said that on a visit to the College Cardinal Giovanni Battista Montini, the future Pope Paul VI, foresaw a future for Maynooth along similar lines to Louvain. This would integrate the seminary training of priests into an open university system. Already it was evident that preparing priests to minister for the Ireland of the future would demand that quality of formation. There was bound to be a benefit in having clerical and lay students educated side-by-side in an atmosphere of mutual respect.

The task of heading up the expansion fell to Monsignor Jeremiah Newman, President of the College, later Bishop of Limerick. It is fair to say that if he had not existed someone like him would have needed to be invented. He thought big and planned forward. It was due to him principally that the adjoining land of sixty-eight acres was acquired from the Lanigan-O'Keeffe estate. The cost then was in the region of £1,000 per acre. It was that land which provided the site for the cluster of class halls, reading rooms with canteens and other facilities that became the New Campus. President Newman also attracted many religious congregations to establish accommodation for their own members and other students around that New Campus. A pedestrian bridge over the intersecting Maynooth–Galway road provides access to the John Paul II Library and the Old Campus.

Beginning with a token lay presence in 1970 the numbers of lay students have since multiplied. Clerical students have continued to decline at an increasing rate over recent years and are now counted in tens rather than in the hundreds of earlier days. As against that more and more lay students are coming to Maynooth for qualifications in Theology. This has led to a major expansion in the B.A. Theology degree where candidates take a joint programme in Arts and Theology. That qualifies students for teaching religion, for school chaplaincy and other forms of lay ministry. Unquestionably this proves to be a major development in terms of professional lay participation in Irish Church life.

During my final years in Maynooth I served as Dean of the Faculty of Theology. The Faculty undertook the validation of programmes of study in various seminaries around the country. Up to that time seminarians would have been studying theology in those centres for four years without any third level recognition. That was unacceptable in a world where such formal recognition provided solid evidence of achievement. Those centres subsequently welcomed lay participants into the programmes. One of the anomalies of working towards degrees in theology at that time was that student grants were not provided by the Irish State. The Department of Finance cited the 1904 University Act and the Irish Constitution, both of which were effectively challenged as inapplicable to the case. The anomaly was underlined by the funding made available for theology studies in Trinity College in Dublin. The anomaly has since been resolved.

It was certainly an exciting time to have a role in the development of the new Maynooth. It has been said that the Trustees launched out without knowing where the prevailing currents would lead into the future. The same might well be said of us on the ground. We were subject to winds and tides outside of our control. It was a matter of availing of opportunities as they presented. Naturally there were *laudatores temporis acti*. They longed to preserve old ways but on the whole there was a strong *esprit de corps* which favoured going forward. If those first crucial steps had not been taken it is impossible to guess what the consequences for Maynooth would have been. One now takes pride in that university town which has grown up on the borders of Dublin. Given the speed of house building it will not be able to age gracefully as Oxbridge has done. Still, with the Dublin–Galway by-pass now in place it will enjoy some measure of tranquillity. If the Trustees had lacked courage in launching out into the future imagine what the later recriminations would have been.

– THE NEW ZEALAND EXPERIENCE –

The most interesting and most enjoyable of my theological forays outside of Ireland were two sessions in New Zealand through the summers of 1975 and 1979. The sessions spread over ten weeks or so with a series of conferences to priests, religious, teachers and doctors. It was a full programme and it required a good deal of work in advance. That advance work paid off handsomely later because it allowed time to get around the country and leisure to meet people. The Gaels and the Kiwis had a similar approach to life. We were both easygoing and good-humoured. Hospitality came naturally to them. They were keen to learn about Ireland and about Europe. They felt isolated. Consequently their young people at the first opportunity would travel abroad, exchange camper vans with groups returning after their round trips and spend a few months on the road through Europe. It reminds one of the Grand Tour of Victorian times.

New Zealand is literally on the other side of planet Earth. My first journey took a full twenty-four hours in a Comet airliner over the Arctic Circle. I felt fine on arrival and brushed aside suggestions that one needed an interval to acclimatise and recover from jet lag. What a mistake! Even though I had slept through some stages on the flight there was a delayed reaction of overpowering tiredness. I have always wondered since how Pope John Paul II succeeded in taking up his punishing schedules of work after those marathon flights of his! I was told afterwards that if you fly west with the sun your biological clock adjusts more readily. That seemed to work second time around.

In a short while I was into the conference programme. The audiences were inspiring, with lively exchanges of views from the floor. The challenges which had confronted Ireland in the wake of the Second Vatican Council were also current in New Zealand. What impressed me was their vibrant sense of mission. Of course, the Catholic Church was in the minority in New Zealand. It had been marginalised by the political might of Presbyterians and Anglicans for over a century. The Catholics were now more than equal to the challenge with lay leadership emerging in many areas. They had a clear feeling that the future was in their hands and that they had work to do. Other Christian traditions there meanwhile remained rooted in the past.

When I got around to the South Island the place names told the story of a Presbyterian tradition with links to Scotland. Dunedin, Invercargill, Stirling and other such town names reflected that. There was still a strong Sabbatharian policy in force in many areas there, much as in Northern Ireland, with businesses and places of recreation closed on Sunday. There was a story, which may have been an urban myth, that a hiker had offered money for milk to a farmer's wife on a Sunday. She declined to touch it but proposed that he leave it on the mantelpiece from where she would lift it on the Monday.

I had the good fortune to be welcomed by two outstanding priests of the Auckland Diocese, Ernie Simmons and Eugene O'Sullivan. Ernie was a historian and brother to Dave, the Director of Auckland Museum. Eugene, native of Glanmire in Cork, chaplain to Auckland University, was a poet and philosopher. Follow that for choice of hosts!

Ernie introduced me to Maori culture with its extraordinary richness in understanding nature. On a visit to Rotorua, the national Maori centre, he showed me through an Anglican church, built on the lines of a Wharepuni, the traditional meeting house of a Maori village. It was a revelation on how religious inculturation could succeed where there was heart and vision. On backgrounds of black basket weave called *tuku-tuku* you had the dynamic symbols favoured by Maori culture. The white vertical line stood for Rangi, Lord of Heaven. The white herringbone horizontal line, the *oku-oku* or arm-pit symbol, carried the triple meaning of the Paschal Mystery: Christ stretching out his arms on the Cross as a hero dying on the field of battle; Christ working with his hands in the role of Redeemer; Christ rowing home over the sea to his heavenly Father. Behind that final symbol was the belief that the spirits of the dead roosted on Cape Reinga, the far tip of the North Island, on an ancient pohutukawa tree, a giant poinsettia, until sunset touched the sea. Then they streamed over the burnished sea path home to Hawaiki, heartland of the Polynesian people.

Ernie and Dave Simmons were both expert on the interpretation of Maori symbolism. The name of every tree and flower had a story to tell. Each physical feature may have owed its title to some event in the Maori creation narrative. Imagine how St Patrick would have incorporated all that in making the Gospel real in the original Aotearoa, the Land of the Long White Cloud! The Maori spiritual ethos surely qualified for what our early missionary theology knew as *anima naturaliter Christiana*, the naturally Christian spirit. Their key values were loyalty to one's family and clan, hospitality for the stranger, peace among those who lived by justice. In a way it reflected something of the ideal philosophy of our Fianna: 'Gloinne ár gchroi, neart ár ngéag and beart do réir ár mbriathar.'

Ernie explained that the French Marist missionaries, who first arrived in New Zealand under Bishop Pompallier, were sensitive to Maori culture. His *Instruction pour les Travaux de la Mission*, written in 1841, is a model for the missionary process of inculturation. He realised that the Maoris would find Christian ideas difficult to assimilate and that the challenge was to build on the good things already found in the Maori way of life. Maori customs should be judged on a relative scale of toleration. This sensitivity remained true for later generations of Dutch Marists. These had certainly informed themselves on Maori spiritual ideas and practices. The success of the New Zealand mission in those early days is quite amazing. The Maori tribes welcomed the missionaries even though these were all Europeans. Because of the long years of training required for Catholic priesthood it is only very recently that Maori and other Polynesian island people progress to ordination. Here, other churches with shorter training periods had a head start.

In a number of recent debates on radio and television in Ireland critics have blamed the Irish missionary system for dismissing the principles of inculturation as followed by St Patrick in Ireland. It is said that we favoured transplanting

St Colman's College, Fermoy
Leaving Certificate Class, June 1949

Ordination, Maynooth 1956

Dunboyne House, Maynooth 1957

On appointment to Maynooth, 1958

Maynooth College Staff, 1967

Meeting with Pope John Paul II, Rome, 1987

'Choosing the flies', Killarney, 1988

'Break for Lunch',
Lough Currane, 2000

contemporary Irish culture into new fields of mission. Whatever about other situations this did not happen in New Zealand, at least to any large extent.

We have an outstanding example in the McDonald brothers from Kilkenny. James arrived in Auckland in 1850, followed by Walter in 1856. Both became proficient in Maori language and culture and were legends in their lifetimes – James among the Maoris in Rotorua and Walter among the poor in Auckland. It is reported that James would arrive in Auckland on his black charger with his cloak of bird plumage topped by a chieftain's huia feathers. As blood brother to the paramount chief in Rotorua he would have been an imposing figure. At the Treaty of Waitangi, which ended the Maori Wars, he was trusted to represent the Maori people in the negotiations with the British. On his death he was given the full honours of a Maori funeral in Rotorua.

I took a special interest in the McDonald brothers. It was their nephew, another Walter, who was Professor of Theology in Maynooth in the early years of the last century. He was a man of original mind. He had a stormy career, partly theological, partly political. He tells the story in his *Reminiscences of a Maynooth Professor*. Recently I lodged in the Maynooth archive a copy of relevant documents from the Congregation for the Propagation of the Faith in regard to this Walter.

Next to Ernie Simmons, Eugene O'Sullivan from Glanmire in Co. Cork became a valued friend, a Christian and a gentleman in every respect. I spent many weekends with him in his chaplaincy house at Auckland, where he presided over a varied group of student Maoris and islanders. What a family scene it was! Each of us took on the role of cooking meals in turn. My Irish stew, well peppered and curried, gained approval. Later I cooked in the oven some promising looking fish caught out in the bay. Unrelieved catastrophe, more like a jellied bouillabaisse than an edible meal! To great applause a Maori lad said that the only way to cook harika, as he called it, was to boil it in brine with a firebrick and then suck the brick!

The liturgies over which Eugene presided were exceptional. He was a man of deep spirituality and drew people to express their faith in a personal way. How fortunate those young Christians were to have such a leader! At evening after the meal we would sit around on the lawn under a large totara pine and discuss whatever topics came the way. Even though it counted as winter in the southern hemisphere, Auckland was close enough to the Equator to have warm sunny days. When darkness fell, without a twilight period, frost set in. That put an end to discussion. Else you were in serious injury time with a chill threatening. It is something about which tourists had to be on guard.

Eugene had great regard for the Maori poet James K. Baxter. He might qualify as the Kiwi Patrick Kavanagh, with the same lack of reverence for all establishments. The ordinary events of day-to-day life with the native flora and fauna were Baxter's stock-in-trade. Now and again he would pick up on some spiritual theme and write a hymn to the Creator, not unlike our Gaelic monks of olden times. The New Zealand countryside lent itself to these spiritual transports. I remember reading his poems on the chaplaincy balcony on a glorious Sunday morning as Auckland harbour was criss-crossed with billowing spinnakers of every colour of the rainbow. It is not for nothing that the boy is known as Waitamata, the shining water. My last meeting with Eugene was when we went together to visit Innisfallen Island in Killarney. The Annals of Innisfallen spoke of the ancient faith of the Gaels. Shortly afterwards he went to join them.

New Zealand would be my first choice of home after Ireland. It is a charmed land. Where else would you hear the single clear note of the bell-bird and the effort of the tui to mimic it? Where else would you find the perfect acoustics of the Waitomo 'cathedral' vault in a cave lit by glow-worms? Where else would you find the twin pristine lakes of

Manipouri-Tyana, their sparkling waters filtered by drifts of pumice stone ringing the shores like a jade garland? I visited Manipouri-Tyana with a group of Irish Mercy sisters from the Convent at Green Island in Dunedin. The sun rolled back the mist as we descended into the valley. Imagine a curtain being raised on a panorama where nature presented its full glory. Then, of course, there was the fishing in the Lake Taupo system. Wild lake trout and rainbows about which I still dream.

During that second visit in 1979 I had discussed plans to exchange roles for a few years with a colleague who was teaching Moral Theology in Mossgiel College in Dunedin. Then it was announced that Pope John Paul II was due to take in Maynooth on his visit to Ireland. For that it was straight home and all hands to work to get everything set up for the occasion, and what an occasion it was! What an extraordinary experience on that autumn morning as the helicopter came to land on the High Field. We shouldered Archbishop Marcinkus, the Pope's handler, to one side. The only concern for him was to get the Pope out and away to Limerick. As it was, the Pope took his time as he walked through the College and met priests, religious and students from all over Ireland. It certainly was a momentous day in Maynooth. The John Paul II Library commemorates it appropriately.

Back in 1979 I said *au revoir* to New Zealand in a monsoon-like downpour. The Maori family with whom I had been staying sent a telegram before take-off: *Roimata ua roimata tangata*, which roughly translates 'the tears of the sky our tears for you'. In those few months in New Zealand I came to know so many people. The memories have not faded. The Irish have certainly left their mark there, particularly in the field of education. One of the religious groups with a high profile were the 'Brown Josephs'. They once had a noviciate in Newmarket in what is now the James O'Keeffe Institute. Two of my O'Callaghan cousins from Taur had entered the congregation. I stayed with Brigid and Lucy at their retreat centre in Mission Bay with unparalleled views of Auckland's Waitamata Bay. Even though they had been seldom home they knew more about my immediate family than I knew myself. It is not the first time that this has happened to me.

New Zealand enthralled me. Everything about it affected me – culture, language, countryside, people. Years later, when in Mallow, I came to know well a Marist priest from New Zealand, Fr Chris Skinner. An outstanding singer, he has recorded many hymns and songs, some of them in Maori. Meeting with him has kept the Maori association alive for me. His gift for composing and recalling tunes has enlivened many a session. He claims that there must be some primeval link between Ireland and New Zealand, particularly in terms of our songs. The evidence is thin though when he heard the Irish hymn *A Mhuire Mhathair* he immediately identified it as a native Maori tune. Of course, New Zealand has also changed. With the rise of the European Union traditional trade links with Europe have now moved east, principally to Japan. Unfortunately, too many young people have looked to places like San Francisco for their social life. This has been a corrupting influence against which a stable Victorian society did not have a defence. However, I still dream about those halcyon days of the seventies.

– THE HUMAN SIDE OF MAYNOOTH LIFE –

It is all too easy to become institutionalised in college. Early in my days in Maynooth I was inspired by a business friend to make a policy decision on a set programme of life. It was a simple enough pattern. When in college organise your day to get the work done. Do not just think about doing it, just do it. I cannot claim that I always followed that rule of life but it certainly remained the prevailing pattern. Otherwise one might spend hours literally just passing time or thinking about work. Then one would feel dissatisfied with little to show for the day. I do not take credit under the head of virtue for that work ethic. It was self-fulfilling. With work done you could strike out to make something worthwhile of the remaining time. Thank God, I never lacked for energy. One can see then how a break from college work would be welcome. I always had gun dogs. At first they were pointers, Grouse and Jeff. Pointers were ideally suited to ranging the open terrain around Maynooth and to the rough shooting on the margins of the Bog of Allen, just a few miles to the west. The college lands and the farms around Carton House always carried a good stock of pheasant. The shooting was just too easy.

The margins of the Bog of Allen were more interesting. I have happy memories of an old friend and sportsman, Joe Mullaly of Donadea. His farm had fingers of rough land running into the bog. With patches of oats and turnips there were pheasants a plenty. Further into the bog there were duck and woodcock. It was a cornucopia of game but we severely limited our bags. On a recent visit to Maynooth I found that most of the best land in Kildare around Carton House is now under houses. The terrain of the Bog of Allen is still much the same except that the game has fallen victim to the inroads of poachers.

At that time I had already begun to question the practice of fowling as a sport. I know that there was a romantic air about that old fashioned picture of man with gun and dog striding across the moor as the grouse season opened on the morning of August 12. But birds are just so beautiful flying wild and free in their native environment. Why reduce them to a scatter of feathers? This applied particularly to wild pheasants. These game birds are territorial and hold their ranges as of right. Shooting them is a kind of piracy. Worse than that, it can feel like sacrilege.

I recall how it ended for me on that glorious January morning when God was in his heaven and all was right with the world. From under a holly bush the dogs flushed a cock pheasant, an old warrior that had survived many a day. Every feather glinted as he rose into the sun crowing a challenge to the world.

As I have explained earlier I did not have similar scruples about angling. Even if I had any such emotional sensitivity it would have been brushed aside as a necessary concomitant to the companionship I enjoyed with close friends in the angling fraternity. My first introduction to the great midland lakes of Ennell and Sheelin was through Fr Mattie Coleman, who was then teaching at St Finnian's College in Mullingar. My Maynooth colleague Brendan Devlin and I had many a glorious day with him on those lakes. Later when Fr Mattie moved to the parish of Carnaross near Kells I would join him for weekends, help out with the work in the parish and fish Lough Sheelin on Sunday evening. In that break to draw breath all stresses evaporated and I returned to Maynooth with a light heart and a fresh mind.

It was through the common interest in angling that I came to know a trio who became my closest and life-long friends. Bishop Eamonn Casey and those ordained with him in Maynooth were celebrating their silver jubilee in Bettystown, Co Meath, in June 1976. I was invited over to speak on current issues in pastoral theology. I had already come to know well Frank O'Leary, a Columban priest from Kerry who had been a student with me in Rome. In Bettystown I met his brother Fr Sean O'Leary. It was through him that I came to know Fr John O'Keeffe, later Dean of Tralee, and Daniel O'Connell, retired ESB linesman. We were a combination of personalities, different as individuals but surely a partnership made in heaven.

After the jubilee class had scattered, the trio joined me and Mattie Coleman on Lough Sheelin where we all bedded down in a Nissan hut on the lake shore planning the morrow. At that time the fishing on the midland lakes was superb as was that in Waterville, which I soon discovered.

Sean O'Leary with John O'Keeffe and another two of the O'Leary brothers, both Columbans, had obtained a cottage over the upper lakes in Waterville in the 1970s. The cottage, in need of total restoration, was acquired for £800 and a freezer!

All hands fell to the task of rebuilding with Sean O'Leary as *chef d'equipe*. That little cottage at Macernane over Lough Eisg-an-Mhactíre became a haven for us and a port of call for all the friends. It would take a volume to do justice to life there.

It proves that the academic commitment can run in tandem with human living. I owe to my friends more than I can ever pay or say. I hope that towards that friendship I have made my contribution. We were inseparable. That trio of special Macernane mates have now crossed the final threshold of life. May the Lord grant them the light of heaven until the day when we hope to meet together in the Communion of Saints. I trust that Peter will have a special welcome for us as 'brothers of the angle', to quote Isaak Walton.

As death claimed most of the original group the little cottage became a lonely place. Actually the unique site with its beautiful scenery still preserved the old happy associations. The loneliness descended when you unlocked the door on that emptiness where once Fr Sean O'Leary had presided like a prince in his house welcoming all comers. Thanks to a white knight in the person of an English angling friend, Michael Gass, who purchased the property, the cottage has been sensitively restored to a standard beyond anyone's appreciation of its potential. I now feel welcome there as ever I did. Michael Gass shares many interests in the countryside. He has named the cottage *Genius Loci*, the spirit place. It certainly has an aura of celebrating nature in all its changing moods as the west wind brushes the mist off the mountain and ruffles the dark surface of the lake. Lough Eisg-an-Mhactíre, usually abbreviated in speech to Lough-na-hEisge, translates as lake of the wolf's ravine. That slash in the face of the mountain opposite runs a cataract in a rainstorm. That adds to the aura of *Genius Loci*.

All this has taught me how little we need from life. On the human level one does well if you enjoy a reasonable measure of health, have the support of a family, be surrounded with a few good friends – and have a reason to get up in the morning. On the health side I have been extraordinarily blessed. It is over sixty years since I was hospitalised with that broken ankle when in St Colman's College in Fermoy. In the meantime I have shaken off a few chills without spending a day in bed. I thank the Lord for that rude good health. Under God the credit must go to the genes I have inherited and to growing up in a healthy environment which has continued in an active outdoor life. Over the years of working with others I have come to appreciate how difficult it is to achieve one's potential where poor health saps energy. The Roman satirist Juvenal summed it up in a telling comment two thousand years ago: *Haud facile emergunt quorum virtutibus obstant res angustae domi.* It is not easy to make one's mark in the world when one's talents are stymied at source.

To health I will add the support of an extended happy family, good neighbours and kind friends. There will have been ups and downs in life but with family and community on call one is never isolated. This support is real social capital often ignored because it does not cash out in economic terms. Back in the sixties when I was still a student it was fashionable to discuss existentialism and analyse the concept of estrangement, alienation and nihilism. The term to conjure with then was *Angst* – boredom with life, ennui, melancholy.

Well, they were happy days when those were just concepts to be analysed over coffee in a university canteen! Today the concepts have become real with a vengeance in a world without direction where youth feels lost. William Wordsworth's 'I wandered lonely as a cloud' is no longer romantic fantasy when one feels lost and rootless. That was never our experience.

Along with family and neighbours one counts friends. Family and neighbours are given. Friends select themselves and are there by mutual choice. I have already mentioned a number of such priest friends. Among others there were very many good people with whom one had passing acquaintance. One trusts that both sides gained from the experience. Then, I have a small number of close lay friends who have literally become part of life.

What I owe them is beyond measure in terms of emotional support in times of joy and sadness. As friends we take one another for granted. We are there for each other. We do not spend time analysing our relationship. With one another we feel at home and can share personal thoughts and ideas. We do not need to wear masks or make constant efforts to impress. That easy level of bonding while respecting due limits not alone facilitates the celibate life but gives human quality to it. True friends affirm one's commitment to the life one has chosen. Who wants to become an emotional prune? Anyway who would identify with that kind of person in the pastoral context? As one assesses the impact of Jesus on the people who came to follow him one appreciates that his genuine humanity must have been a major influence.

Talking about a reason to get up in the morning brings me also to Jesus. I do not here intend to preach about the general theology of vocation and ministry. I confine myself to personal experience. Even at the human level one needs a purpose in life for personal fulfilment. With the addition of its Christian motivation I have found that personal purpose in living and working as a priest. There have been difficult and stressful times when getting up in the morning has opened on a sky of unrelieved grey. Then I pray 'Jesus, I place my trust in you'. As Pope John Paul II said: 'Jesus did not come down from the Cross.' It would be a sign of a poor commitment to a vocation if one were continually weighing up the odds in face of challenges and wondering whether one was up to it.

In the report of Justice Frank Murphy on child sex abuse in the Diocese of Ferns the issue of clerical celibacy was raised. An expert group of therapists had given their unanimous view that 'the vow of celibacy contributed to the problem of sexual abuse in the Church'. What they intended to target must surely have been the manner in which clerical celibacy was too often perceived and lived rather than the essential nature of the vow of clerical celibacy itself. The spiritual principle at the heart of the Christian commitment to celibacy would have stressed then as now the concept of generous service and positive witness to the values of the Gospel, the vocation to make Christ's kingdom a reality on earth. Unfortunately the culture at the time undermined this positive spiritual principle by the prevailing negative attitude to sexuality. Celibacy was coloured as saying no to marriage. This readily leads to repression of the sexual instinct rather than to its integration as part of human experience. Original sin was invoked to reinforce this. That rejection of sexuality as threatening would have coloured the understanding of clerical celibacy. The express Gospel inspiration for mission was then less motivating for celibacy than the implicit distancing from sexuality.

At first sight one would think that 'the relative loneliness and isolation of the diocesan priesthood' referred to in the Ferns Report would be perceived as the downside of celibacy and set the stage for aberrant behaviour such as child sex abuse. However, as described in the Report, the typical abuser tended to be an outgoing gregarious hail-fellow-well-met. Was this a façade? Was it a way of gaining access to children? Perhaps the abuse was the consequence of an arrogant sense of invulnerability on the part of the abuser. This would have neutralised and disarmed the deterrent factor which would have operated in the case of other people who might have harboured similar tendencies but without the priest's ready access to children.

Looking back on my own time I thank family and close friends for providing a healthy environment in which to live the celibate life. With one or two of those close women friends there was certainly a mutual sexual attraction but we would have been aware of the boundaries. The saving reality is that in a close relationship where each party is committed to living a full life the factor of dependence does not predominate. On the contrary each continues to live one's own life and to be supportive of the other. For this I thank providence that celibacy did not become a personal problem. I will not pontificate about how others succeed or fail in their commitment. Life is a tangled skein. When one does fail it is honest and Christian to accept that fact rather than expect others to approve. An understanding and forgiving spirit does not imply approval.

CHAPTER 4

THE CALL TO PARISH LIFE

During my time on the staff at Maynooth I had built up some
experience of pastoral life outside the college. My links with
Dublin came through Bishop Peter Birch from the staff at
Maynooth, who had recently been appointed Bishop of
Ossory. He asked me to take on the role of chaplain to Our
Lady of Knowledge praesidium of the Legion of Mary in
North Great George's Street with which he had been
associated. It was an active praesidium with the majority of
members drawn from the Dublin civil service.

At that time in the early sixties the Legion was a spiritual
powerhouse involving in its mission so many people of
extraordinary vision and commitment. It was inspiring to
observe the earnestness of the members in carrying through the
programme of prayer and work set out in the Legion
Handbook. Those praesidium meetings opening with prayer
around the image of Our Lady really fostered Christian faith.
I have happy memories of that and of the camaraderie among
the group. Then we had the Patrician conferences organised by
the Legion on a variety of topics open to all comers. That and
the Viatores Christi, who went out on temporary mission over
summer, were all part of the Legion outreach.

The Second Vatican Council with its pastoral orientation
should have provided an opportunity for a renewed vision, a
new launching into the deep. In hindsight it is seen that
commitment to a tightly knitted system delayed the process for

the Legion. Speculation about the direction the Council was taking provided a motive for circling the wagons in the trust that when the turmoil had passed the new ideas would merge with the accepted wisdom. Our praesidium had the first indication of this holding policy when we submitted to headquarters an agenda for a Curia congress following on broad consultation as to what were the major challenges arising from the Vatican Council for the Irish Church. Our submission was turned down and a selection of agenda from former conferences was forwarded for our consideration as templates. In the event the topics set for discussion allowed for a broader analysis of issues. Loyalty to Legion discipline could also be creative!

The founder of the Legion, Frank Duff, had himself been an observer at the Council where the assembled bishops acclaimed him. He wished Legion members to appreciate that the positive pastoral concerns addressed in Rome had already found the means of answering them through the experience of the Legion system. This protectionist policy did not prove convincing to our praesidium. We knew that other praesidia were also concerned to plan into the future and to have the issues raised by the Council discussed. This concern gradually came to set the tone in many Dublin praesidia.

Concilium is the central council which represents the Legion worldwide. An t-Athair Donncha O'Floinn, then Parish Priest of Bray and one-time Professor of Irish in Maynooth, was the respected and much loved chaplain to Concilium. With a period in hospital in the offing he proposed that I take on the role of chaplain temporarily and he suggested a method on how to promote discussion on ways forward for the Legion. He was a very shrewd judge. He knew that the initiative would not come from Frank Duff nor from those close to him. There were on the ground at Concilium a considerable group who wished to see the handbook better organised and a fresh orientation given to both structure and ministry as reflecting the theological and pastoral insights of the Council. Seamus

Grace from Dún Laoghaire, highly respected by the Legion rank and file, took a leading role. In spite of their efforts it did not prove possible to move this concern up the Concilium agenda. I was glad when An t-Athair Donncha returned even though his improvement in health did not last long.

It would have been evident to everyone, even to Frank Duff himself, that the handbook called out for some revision. It had accumulated piecemeal additions over the years with little regard for logical sequence. The delay in undertaking the revision would seem to have been the concern that the Legion system itself would in the process come up for reassessment. In a specific foreword to the handbook there was a clear policy statement against any alteration of the Legion system. There was also a chapter titled 'The Legion System Invariable' which states: 'Each variation, however slight, makes others inevitable, till presently a body is in existence which indeed bears the name, but possesses little else of the Legion.' That left little space for the pastoral dynamic flowing from the Council which should have found a ready response from a group as inspired as the Legion certainly was.

The ways of Providence are indeed strange. Frank Duff as founder of the Legion of Mary was certainly inspired. He had the vision and commitment required to launch a new pastoral initiative. As one reads about those early years one recognises the power of the Spirit in his work and in that of the group which gathered around him. Without that strong leadership and that vision in setting out a programme of work and prayer the Legion of Mary would have been just another marginal movement in the lay apostolate. As it was it marked out a headline worldwide. It does not take from Frank to admit that he may not have been the man for all seasons. He would appear to have lacked the flexibility required for reading the signs of the times, of which Pope John XXIII had spoken at the outset of the Council, when those signs did not favour the strong views he maintained based on past experience. The question was about the exclusive relevance of that past experience to the challenges which were now confronting the Church after Vatican II. In this regard he would have mirrored the thinking of Archbishop John Charles McQuaid, who may well have been the mentor that steadied his hand on the tiller until matters returned to calmer waters.

It is known that at the Council many bishops were of the opinion that there should be a particular document dedicated to the theology of Mary. Whatever about Frank Duff's position on this issue he expressed his happiness that the role of Mary was incorporated into the major foundational Constitution *Lumen gentium*, which set out the theology of the Church. This is how he saw the link: 'Mary is inseparable from the Catholic Church. You cannot take her out and yet leave the Church intact. It would cease to be the Catholic Church. Her position is primary ... the Council insists that all apostleship is but an extension of the motherhood of Mary; it is part of her giving of Christ to the world. It follows that nobody can take part in apostleship or persevere in it except with her.' The inspiration is there. At issue was the will to broaden the perspective of the Legion system. It mirrored the challenge responded to by John the Baptist when he accepted that the ministry of Jesus took priority over his.

It was reported that the French bishops had once considered using the Legion of Mary system as template for the general lay apostolate in France. Frank Duff's response was that they were certainly welcome to employ the experience of the Legion of Mary but that the identity of the Legion in name and system should not be compromised. Apparently some friction remained on this score. On the fiftieth anniversary of the founding of the Legion of Mary a letter of congratulations was sent from Rome signed by Cardinal Veuillot, Secretary of State. The concluding paragraph in the letter, I seem to recall, referred to the need for renewal in the approach of all Church ministries following on Vatican II. One of those close to Frank Duff commented that he saw this as a critical reflection on the Legion emanating personally from that French Cardinal.

Looking back on that offer of close collaboration proposed by the French bishops another factor in Legion policy comes to light. The Legion seems to have kept a distance even from other groups of the lay apostolate in Ireland. This appeared quite early in the Commission established by the Irish Bishops after Vatican II. Here the Legion of Mary should have been at the forefront in identifying opportunities to develop the lay apostolate in response to the new challenges. I suppose it indicates that the same qualities that make for a good founding father may prove an obstacle when it comes to facing the challenge of a radical review. The directing of a well-proven system over a long period of tranquil expansion may prove a barrier to a refocus. The Legion system consciously mirrored that of the structure of the Roman army. That military perception of the plan of campaign may have led to the closing down of options when new challenges emerge.

Looking back on my years with the Legion of Mary I realise what a pioneering movement it was in the ministry of Lay Apostolate. At a time when clerical influence was strongly in the ascendant in Ireland, the Legion was a star in its capacity to inspire lay people to participate in active Church ministry. The movement was essentially directed by its lay leadership. The priest acted in the role of chaplain. Vatican II with its stress on the ministry of lay people in the mission of the Church would have provided a God-sent opportunity for that worldwide lay movement which the Legion certainly was. Here Ireland had an inspired system in place, well-proved on the ground. It had the pastoral experience and the credibility. It could have run parallel to the long-established missionary outreach for which Ireland was celebrated. It could have acted as lay arm of that clerical/religious outreach. Imagine what a welcome there would have been for a movement of this quality to give direction to the international lay apostolate as inspired with the pastoral incentive of Vatican II! The Legion had already proved that it could apply its basic system to various cultures. Imagine what the commitment and vision of that younger Frank Duff could have achieved in the Kairos presented by this new pastoral challenge! 'The wind of the Spirit blows as it wills. No one knows from whence it comes or whither it goes.'

The extraordinary work of envoys such as Edel Quinn and Charlie Lambe in spreading the Legion of Mary internationally will continue to amaze historians of religion. The question that needs to be asked is whether the Legion should then have drawn on that international pool of expertise to guide the process of evangelisation here. Ireland, where the central Legion authority was based, had remained something of a backwater. I do not recall that Frank Duff visited the Legion envoys in their missionary territories overseas. What he was hearing about the work at second hand would have been a poor substitute for personal experience. It is easy to analyse with hindsight about the what-might-have-beens on the fronts of structures and procedures. What I wish to put on record above all else is the quality of so many individual Legionaries in carrying out their ministries week-in week-out. They could not have achieved this without a structure. Still, structures like people can suffer hardening of the arteries, particularly when the structures become criteria for assessing initiatives. None of this takes from the sanctity of Frank Duff. He is a star in the Christian firmament. When all is said and done in human terms he remains a man of his times. He could be no other. In everything he was true to his Christian convictions, and they were admirable.

It was during the 1916 celebrations in 2006 that this came home to me. On the back of the Legion handbook there is that deeply religious poem of Joseph Mary Plunkett: 'I see his blood upon the rose and in the stars the glory of his eyes.' The poet was among the fifteen patriots executed in Kilmainham Gaol at Easter in 1916. Another of the same religious character was Tomas McDonagh, one-time teacher in St Colman's College in Fermoy. The plaque that commemorates him in that college carries the legend composed by none other than An t-Athair

Donncha O'Floinn: 'Innis fós go mairid Gael', to the effect that the true spirit of the Gael still flourishes.

Is it not a fair assessment that they both shared the idealism of those patriots who were inspired by the vision of an Ireland for which they were prepared to die? Frank Duff wrote a pamphlet entitled *True Devotion to the Nation*. It is a very personal witness, redolent of the idealism of those he surely admired, even though names are not mentioned. Like William Bulfin, of whom I have already spoken, Frank Duff travelled all over Ireland on his trusty bicycle. He saw at first hand that we were not living up to the challenges of our hard-bought freedom. To correct this he invoked the Christian ideal of the Mystical Body to inspire a sense of genuine community and respect for our homeland for which we had the privilege and duty of loving care as Irish citizens.

I made good friends in the Legion of Mary. One such, President of the original Praesidium in North Great George's Street, has over the years provided me with a home from home in Dublin. One is blessed to meet one such special person in the course of life. As a true friend should always do she never hesitated to confront me with home truths where others would have been diffident about speaking their minds. Given the pedestal on which families place their priest they may leave him with a false persona. It is invaluable to have someone on hand, as St Paul said, 'speaking the truth in love'.

It was through the Legion of Mary that I came into contact with some priests in Dublin. On many Sundays I would celebrate Mass in one of the city parishes. I have happy memories of Mass in Meath Street in the inner city. The Liberties was then a live community layered across three generations. Grandparents saw to it that youngsters did not become involved in vandalism or in any form of mayhem. They were a lovely people and so supportive of one another. I remember that if there was a call to attend to someone who asked for the Last Sacraments the neighbours would have the room ready and candles lighted. The city planners who moved families out to Ballymun and Finglas little realised that while you may dismantle community with the stroke of a pen it takes generations to establish one.

– APPOINTMENT TO MALLOW –

I have already described my coming to know Mattie Coleman when he was teaching in St Finnian's College in Mullingar. Before he became Parish Priest in Carnaross near Kells he had been appointed administrator in Navan. This was a difficult posting. Navan on the outskirts of Dublin had problems spilling over from the city. Then you had a number of younger men filtering through from the North more or less on the run from police or paramilitaries. If you add in the camp followers from Tara Mines you had an explosive mixture if anyone struck a spark. You can well imagine what a relief it was for Mattie Coleman to be appointed to the rural parish of Carnaross in the heart of Meath. For him it was paradise. For me it became a source of the happy memories which I have described above. It was also a good introduction to parish life. In the stream of day-to-day life in Maynooth the years were passing without giving time for much thought about where one was headed. In the autumn of 1982 I was in Mallow for the funeral of the Parish Priest, Canon Willie Buckley, who had been just a few months in the post. On returning to Maynooth Bishop John Ahern telephoned me with the oblique comment that some of the priests believed that with Mallow vacant it might be decision time for me. I heard that this option had been aired during the funeral. I had already given thought to it on the way back to Maynooth. At the age of fifty it should be decision time for a change of direction if that is in prospect at all.

I told the Bishop that I welcomed the appointment and looked forward to meeting the challenge but that I would need some months to organise the situation in Maynooth to cover the areas for which I was directly responsible. I would have left the Department of Moral Theology in disarray if I had moved on just at the start of the academic year. In my letter of resignation to the Trustees I wrote 'I leave Maynooth with personal regret but with appreciation of the fact that I was fortunate to spend the greater part of my life in so congenial a home'. I still endorse that in memory twenty-five years later. It did not prove possible to make alternative arrangements for the Medical Ethics module in UCD. I decided to commute and cover the programme by clustering the sessions early in each week. That very good friend of many years close by the University, in whose home I was always welcome, provided the overnight accommodation. This was a welcome factor in easing the change to Mallow and the distancing from so many friends, even though I appreciated from my earlier associations there that Mallow would also be a congenial place. It had little in common with Navan except for similarity in size!

I had not realised that the prospect of distancing oneself from lifelong friends could be so traumatic. I saw myself as missing particularly the camaraderie of Maynooth and the closeness of an O'Callaghan family in Dublin with which I had bonded. In that home full of lively children I had come to realise how much one misses in terms of family life when we spend most of our maturing years in boarding school. Anyway in the event that perception of distancing from friends was not realised. Friendship operated on a different pattern but the quality did not suffer. As it turned out immersion in parish work with challenges a plenty would leave little time for nostalgia.

Come Christmas I had transferred to Mallow. I was already familiar with the general situation because some members of my family had their homes there. Having them close made the transition easier. In the parish there were very experienced priest colleagues, Bobby Forde and Tom McSweeney. Coincidentally both of them had been teachers over many years in St Colman's College in Fermoy. Their advice proved invaluable in putting a newcomer in the pastoral picture. I had so much to learn and I never questioned their judgement.

When first appointed I had a call from Niall Crowley, AIB Chairman, whose uncle Fr Tim Crowley had baptised me in Meelin. Niall himself had been a guiding force in organising funding for the John Paul II Library in Maynooth. He told me that he had done some background research on Mallow and had discovered that it did not have a central office for the administration of so large a parish. On the need for this he was adamant. Buy it or build it, he said. Otherwise a parish priest would spend so much time in day-to-day administration that one would be busy non-stop with little worthwhile to show for it apart from maintaining a system. When our team of priests got together there was little need to make the case.

They agreed that the vacant Georgian presbytery building at Bank Place was the ideal location for a parish centre, right across the road from St Mary's Church. Done then, but now arose the matter of funding the restoration and adaptation. There was already a debt of £70,000 on the parish arising from the building of replacement presbytery accommodation. It had been intended to sell the vacant presbytery to pay off this debt. The priests said that Bishop Ahern would be unlikely to advance from the diocese the large loan now required. I do not recall the source of the suggestion that we should request loans from some parishes which were cash rich. The parishes responded immediately. It certainly was a vote of confidence. The agreement was that Mallow would remit to them the current bank deposit interest and that the loans could be called in at any time.

The vacant presbytery amounted to two side-by-side houses of three stories over basement. It was an impressive building. It now seems quite incredible that £65,000 was the highest offer tendered for it when on sale. The budget for the upgrade of the Bank Place building was set at £150,000. The support for the project from the parishioners was overwhelming. Naturally there were some complaints that the ex-academic would pauperise the parish! We were blessed that Canon Willie Buckley, with his superb pastoral vision and sensitivity, had already launched the weekly envelope collection in the parish. The response removed all concern about meeting not just the amount of the outstanding £70,000 loan but the cost involved in the work on the parish centre. One parishioner who generously volunteered invaluable assistance was our architect, the late Patrick O'Keeffe. He was a calm presence when any panic threatened.

In the process of upgrading we had some heart-stopping moments. After the Stardust tragedy in Dublin, fire officers had become extra-vigilant in regard to places of public assembly. The fire safety report on the planned parish centre would have required an extra spend of £45,000! A fire lobby around one stairwell; two covered fire escapes up the back elevation; and a fire exit through the gable to the adjoining lane! Fortunately, in a superb display of lateral thinking, one young apprentice worker on the site proposed that as the two houses were divided by a common three foot thick wall, each house with internal fire doors fitted could act as a fire escape for its neighbour. That left the fire officer astounded at his oversight.

That centre has proved its worth many times over in the service it has provided to parish and community. The location is ideal on the main street beside the principal town car park and the Garda headquarters. It is right beside St Mary's Church. At the beginning we were wondering what use we would make of an extensive three storey over basement Georgian building. That question has certainly taken care of itself. At the heart of the building beside the main door the parish office is accommodated. There the day-to-day administration takes place and from there the various activities of the parish are organised. Right through the day people call in to make an enquiry or to access some service. The parish secretary has become a source of information not just on all parish activities but on every agency in the town.

The basement houses the heritage centre. This compiles a database of family records for the Diocese of Cloyne. We take particular pride that over the years in co-operation with FÁS, over five hundred trainees there have qualified for permanent employment. This database provides the material from which family histories are supplied to clients. It helps to defray the costs of the heritage centre.

Every square metre of the rest of the building is used in some parochial or community activity. Everyone sees it as essential for the work of the parish. Even more essential than buildings are personnel. When I came to Mallow the key person was the sacristan, Billy Walsh. He was already a legend. He was an indefatigable worker in the parish and in the community. If I were to choose a motto for him it would be 'No sooner said than done'. You could entrust him with anything. Martina Aherne, the first parish secretary, was of a similar nature: competent and conscientious. With those two at the centre of things it was easy to build a team around them, including the caretaker, Billy Sweeney. It was that team spirit that I have treasured above everything else. It is accepted that with priests and assistants in a parish working together as a team any challenge becomes an opportunity.

Mallow has always been blessed in the number of volunteers who are active at all levels in the parish and in the community. Closely connected with the work of the Church there were the Ministers of the Eucharist and of the Word and those who took care of the sanctuary. Then you had the teams of collectors who, Sunday after Sunday, were there to see that the offerings were collected, counted and made ready for banking. Visitors from abroad would comment on the small amounts of individual offerings in Ireland compared to experience in their churches abroad. Still, we were never short of funds to meet day-to-day expenses and to finance major developments. Here the system of weekly envelopes provided a war chest to meet capital commitments. In any town parish it is accepted that at best one third of families contribute to the weekly envelope collection – and indeed support all community projects. In rural parishes, where there is a greater sense of local identity, the percentage would be higher. What I do say is that we in Mallow were never called on to delay any worthwhile project because of lack of finance.

– THE SCHOOL SCENE –

There was a range of primary and secondary schools in Mallow, five at primary level with the later addition of a Gaelscoil, and three at second level. Those schools had over the years a very creditable history in terms of educational achievement and a positive Christian ethos. On this latter front we in Ireland have taken for granted the contribution of teachers in handing on the faith. They should be recognised for what they really are: frontline lay ministers.

The common ministry of home-school-parish in handing on the faith is now recognised. The first express step in that common ministry was the greater focus on First Eucharist preparation through the *Do This in Memory* programme as the new Millennium began. Up to that we had left matters largely to the teachers. With a background in education, and with two generations of teachers before me, I had special interest in the schools. I quickly came to recognise the nature and the extent of the commitment made by teachers at both primary and secondary levels. I wish that some of those who criticise would switch places with one of them in the classroom just for a day.

Where there are problems in a pupil's home those frequently tend to surface at school. The lack of a secure ordered home life transfers over. Every child has a right to appropriate education but this requires resources where there are problems. There is more recognition of this today than in the past. It is now appreciated that the earlier the intervention the better the long-term result. What needs better recognition is that a pupil's rights do not exist in isolation. One must surely take account of the rights of others. A disruptive student may not be allowed to compromise the entitlement of the school community to a proper environment for teaching and learning. An ethic of discipline worked out as a code in consultation with all interested parties is thereby an essential.

Parents as a body now see themselves as major stakeholders in the process of education. This is a welcome development and bodes well for the future. Earlier parents' associations were considered mainly as valuable sources of funds. They have advanced to play a role in the management and general development of the schools. In that role, professional associations of parents now take the long-term perspective rather than focus just on the concerns that affect the current cohort of students. The quality of those elected from among the parents on to the Board of Management will promote that professionalism. It is evident that lay people appointed by Trustees and elected by parents will continue into the future to have more responsibility in the management of schools. Traditionally it was taken for granted that a priest or religious would chair a Board of Management. Today on almost every school Board of Management there are lay people well qualified for the role of chair.

In the past the funding of national schools in terms of providing buildings and in contributing capitation amounts for pupils was seen as quite a burden on parishes. Even so, we in Ireland did not appreciate our privileged position. Effectively the national schools were *de facto* denominational from the beginning. The State paid the salaries of teachers and eventually took on the major responsibility for providing accommodation. In other countries the burden of providing and supporting church schools fell directly on the parishes. Even granted our favoured status in Ireland, some parishes found it problematic to provide the contribution to schooling where fewer families practised their faith. Parents who had distanced themselves from the parish were not making contributions. Naturally this was an occasion for grievance.

The situation has eased in recent times by greater financial State support across the board.

For effective catechesis, home, school and parish should be of one voice, each supporting one another in the common purpose of building up the faith of the young person. In today's pluralist culture a secular influence is on the ascendant. It has affected more and more homes, even more radically than what the Irish bishops foresaw in their pastoral letter *Handing on the Faith in the Home* back in 1981. This puts greater pressure on teachers who in times past would accept that children coming to school would have some religious knowledge and actual experience of prayer. In the absence of faith and religious practice in the home one hears of children not coming to Mass after First Communion because they have no one to bring them.

I have already mentioned the commitment of our teachers to the ministry of evangelisation in the schools. This has been taken for granted by parishes as part of a teacher's terms of appointment. It is an area of which parishes now need to take account. Dependence on the contractual duty to teach religion and provide catechesis to young Christians will be a poor basis on which to base and motivate a ministry. Furthermore, many teachers in the contemporary culture will not be practising their faith and may even no longer personally believe. It would be self-evidently prejudicial and hypocritical for them to continue in catechesis, as for parishes to expect them to do so. Already executives in the teachers' unions have been flagging this as a concern. It will come home to us as a concern more quickly than we anticipate. Organising something along the lines of Sunday School in the parish will be a major pastoral responsibility.

The introduction of Religious Studies to the examination programme at second level is a welcome development. It gives direction to the search for meaning and direction of life which should be at the heart of education. Giving religion academic status moves it into the mainstream programme in school. The array of texts now available provides a more informative and imaginative choice of material. When teachers really take the subject to heart their enthusiasm will find a response in the reactions of their students. Religious studies is not the soft option as first perceived. It is a real challenge to the intellect and is welcomed by the more intelligent and philosophically-minded students.

The introduction of religion into the examination syllabus took place after years of discussion on how religious studies and catechesis should relate and on whether or not one would compromise the other. The agreed case now is that they should run in tandem. Religious studies provide a background and broad general context for the study of religion in history and culture. Catechesis has the more personal focus of inspiring faith and of directing a way of life. Here celebration of one's faith goes hand-in-hand with catechetical instruction. The old adage maintains its relevance. *Lex orandi, lex credendi.* The pattern of prayer reflects the pattern of faith.

Collaboration between religion teacher, catechist and chaplain is the key to the success of the overall initiative. In the future these roles will be filled to an increasing extent by lay people. Currently more and more are being qualified at Maynooth College and at Mater Dei Institute. Already there is clear recognition of the support that these posts represent in schools. Where so many students have emotional and other personal problems it is necessary to have a team of resource people on hand to assist them and their families. It speaks well for the regard in which the need for such resources is held that State policy now favours the funding of chaplaincy posts.

One area of education in which I became much involved was that of the Co. Cork Vocational Education Committee. I joined the committee in 1988 and was chairman for a decade. During that time Co. Cork VEC had two outstanding chief executive officers in Bobby Buckley and Barra O'Briain. Under their inspired leadership our committee played a central role among vocational education schemes nationwide when the overall education system was in the process of reorganisation. The recognition of this central role was clear at the annual meetings of the Irish Vocational Education Association which worked out overall future policies. Experience in the VEC taught me a great deal about the need to plan ahead to realise projects and to set down the various steps to achieve results. Every meeting was directed to action. It has rendered me hypersensitive to 'talking shops' where strategies and tactics are discussed *ad nauseam* without solid decisions taken on a time scale.

The VEC system as established in 1930 opened up a broad horizon in its commitment to 'continuing education'. It was intended as an alternative to the academic stream in the secondary schools, which were traditionally managed by church personnel. The VEC schools were then typically dismissed as second class with 'Technical School' dismissively shortened to 'the Tech'. They had also attracted a certain amount of distancing from religious bodies. However, the record shows that from the beginning the Diocese of Cloyne had a priest representative, generally the chairman, on the committee. That bond between Diocese and VEC has been confirmed in the Model Agreement which directly links some VEC colleges with the Diocese.

Without question the Vocational Education system has more than measured up to the expectations of its 1930 founders. On the way it has equalled the academic quality of the secondary school system. Then the concept of 'continuing education' has allowed it to expand in all directions upwards and outwards. It takes pride in having established the Institutes of Technology which now rival the universities. It has pioneered developments in the community from culture to sport. It has established adult and community education on a broad spectrum – craft, music, drama, home management, winter farm schools, night classes in anything and everything where an interest needs to be fostered.

One development which I treasure is that of the Youthreach system. It represents a programme of second-chance education. Its outstanding success in Mallow stands to the credit of the co-ordinators and highly-motivated staff. Morale, team-work and an atmosphere of good humour are what make it a welcoming environment for young people whose experience of standard education may not have been positive

One can see how this broad vision recommended itself to Irish priests who tended to engage themselves in the community. The typical Irish priest was never a 'sacristy priest' who confined his interest to ecclesiastical concerns. Look at those pioneering priests who have left their mark on Irish history as they forged the future of our country. Canon Hayes of Bansha founded Muintir na Tire. Canon McDyer of Glencolumcille breathed new life into the co-operative movement. Canon Horan of Knock established a lifeline to the West through an airport. They blazed a trail for so many others. Today Fr Harry Bohan in Clare is a leading light in the community and has broken new ground in the Céifin Institute in Ennis, which is committed to analysing the directions which Irish society should be taking.

The VEC philosophy envisaged something far wider and richer than formal classroom instruction. A 1970 Department of Education memorandum on Vocational Education directed that 'Distinctive features of national life be carefully fostered' and that it 'should lead to new types of rural occupation and a thoroughly modern rural economy'. The Co. Cork VEC took all this to heart. Its motto is 'Education through Partnership'. 'Ní neart go chur le chéile.' This is the generosity of spirit we need in Ireland, where formerly every strand in our tradition tended to define itself against others. Brendan Behan said that the 'Split' should be the top item on the agenda at the first meeting of any Irish association! That partnership has worked to everyone's benefit through links forged with the Diocese. Among other factors it was this partnership and openness to the future that have made my years on the Co. Cork VEC both a learning experience and a happy memory.

– Engaging with the Media –

Media in one form or other always interested me. The cut and thrust of debate about issues was the spice of life. It exercised the mind and kept one on a learning curve through interacting with other points of view. In the process one honed one's own opinions and geared one up for a more considered response to some challenge.

In this field my daily fare has been principally *The Irish Times*, particularly the letter page covering topics of current interest. The paper also carries informative articles on a variety of issues. It is the national paper of record. One expected from it the more objective account of what someone had actually said on the particular point at issue. The opinions of in-house commentators cannot substitute for that. As the maxim holds, facts are sacred, opinions are free. The opinions of columnists may be relevant but they are typically predictable and in character. The columnists will be selective in their versions and verdicts. Once you allow for that you take their views with the traditional grain of salt.

One may not like the tabloids but you cannot ignore them. They do target the lurid and the sensational but in catering for their chosen common denominator they hold the passing attention of a large audience. The sales figures prove how that policy pays healthy dividends. To counter this commercial challenge editors of the broadsheets inevitably tend to lower their standards in clearing stories for printing. In that process of tabloidisation they will exceed the restraints of traditional codes of ethics beyond what a critical public should be expected to tolerate. Of course, that threshold of tolerance will have been lowered by that same gradual drip-feed of questionable quality.

More honoured in the breach than the observance has been respect for the principle of the NUJ code of conduct which prescribes that only considerations of overriding public interest may be invoked to justify intrusions into private grief and distress. On occasion pressure to lead with a story may reduce concern for public interest into satisfying public curiosity.

John Waters, who frequently plays gadfly to his fellow journalists, summed it up well. 'Nowadays, because of competitive pressures and the increasing trend towards short-term contracts, journalists are conditioned to see themselves more as salespersons handling "product" or entertainers providing diversion, than as custodians of the public interest.' What sparked off his comments were the blatantly false allegations printed about the circumstances in which Liam Lawlor had met his death in Moscow in November 2005.

Those representing church interests over recent years tend to blame the media for bias in coverage of anything in reference to the Catholic Church. In so far as this is true it is in large part a reaction to the oppressive regime of past years, linked with the unwillingness of too many church spokespersons to come on the record with straight comment on some relevant issue. We tend to be so much on our guard that we give the impression that we are hedging and being economical with the truth, forgetting that the impression we make may well be more important than what we say.

The Irish media policy of more recent years has certainly acted as a corrective to the servile attitude which was fostered in times past through excessive respect for the powers-that-be. We live in a very different culture. When media people are challenged on the downside of this culture shift, they may say that they reflect the changes rather than cause them. Along similar lines I recall Gay Byrne's comment that advertising simply fulfilled wants rather than created them. This drew the response that in that case advertisers are throwing their money away.

Whatever one may say, the media has been a driving force in social change. It influences public opinion. While profits may be the bottom line, editors and columnists naturally promote the ideology which they share as a caste. Their policies tend to reflect liberal lines of thinking as a matter of course. Everyone pays lip-service to pluralism but the bias of political correctness skews what is reported and how it is reported.

Political correctness avoids criticism of the prevailing liberal culture. Does that mean that everything goes? Will tolerance then become the only value, the cannibal virtue which consumes the others? Should there then be a rethink about the direction in which the overly tolerant society is going?

In November 2004 Ombudsman Emily O'Reilly addressed the question at the high powered Céifin conference in Ennis. She had once been a champion of the liberal front. In a sobering analysis she now expressed major concerns about the direction in which Ireland was headed. She was unhappy about the spiritual malaise and the absence of positive values in the mindset of the new generation. In a moral vacuum how do you initiate children into a responsible way of life?

The media fulfils an essential purpose in a democracy as voice for the people. It casts a critical eye over the policies and actions of those who manage society. They should be guardians of the public interest. The question then arises: *Quis custodiet ipsos custodes*? Who then guards the guardians? This concern was brought centre stage in the aftermath of the Liam Lawlor episode and of the cartoons of Muhammed which proved so offensive to Islam. Invoking a right to free expression as an absolute does not justify irresponsibility. In any action one is responsible for the foreseeable consequences.

To secure proper standards one would welcome a form of self-censorship, so that an accepted *esprit de corps* could prove effective as a measure of monitoring. In the UK the Press Complaints Commission acts as a self-regulatory body established to uphold a Code of Practice, agreed with the industry. For personal and party reasons politicians currently tend to favour the option of statutory control. Democracy would be the loser where this compromises the independence of the media.

I like the cut-and-thrust of public debate. In regard to issues of Church concern we in Ireland in one regard have been poorly served in contrast to Britain. There, lay people share debates and enter the lists side by side with clergy. The letter pages in *The Tablet* are always a joy to read. So are the British broadsheets generally. Perhaps we priests in Ireland have not given lay people the space or the self-confidence to present their views. In the debate on the various issues around child sex abuse a better balance would have been achieved if more informed lay people had expressed their judgements. Among the rules of equity the central principle is *Audiatur altera pars*: let the other side be heard. Priests and religious do not have the necessary credibility in representing what might show the Church in a more balanced light. They would promptly attract the comment: 'Isn't that what you expect from them!' Informed lay people should join the lists in any public debate.

– WRITING FOR *THE CORKMAN* –

When I came to Mallow I was keen to engage with local media and write at a more popular level than what I had been doing in specialised theological journals. Of its nature that kind of writing tends to be abstract and for a small coterie of academics, what the French call *une science de cabinet*. It was my classmate from Meelin, John Joe Brosnan, then editor of *The Corkman*, who proposed that I subscribe a column. That was in 1986. That *Corkman* column still continues to appear week after week, now numbering a thousand or more. The flow of writing now runs on autopilot as the deadline clicks in every Thursday. Once I have interest in a topic and have given thought to it, putting it on paper does not take a great effort.

When I scan the list of topics over those twenty years it presents a patchwork of everything under the sun. There will be issues of current interest in Church and State, items on religion, historical sketches, country lore and whatever you're having yourself! The one essential is that the topic be of interest to readers. Being reduced to pot-boiling just to fill space would kill the enjoyment in communicating one's ideas. Both I and the readers would switch off.

Where do the ideas come from? Perhaps one reads something in book, magazine, or newspaper which gets you thinking. Perhaps some debate on radio or television holds the attention. Perhaps you meet someone on the street who makes a suggestion. That interchange with readers makes it all worthwhile. It gives a good feeling to the work of writing. In times past local papers such as *The Kerryman* or *The Corkman* were not seen as serious players in the media scene. They passed as light weight, not meriting a second glance from anyone apart from those with an interest in local gossip. This has changed in fact and in perception. The increasing circulation reflects a higher quality of content and more general appeal. This has attracted big media players such as UTV to add to their media empires by purchasing local papers for considerable sums.

The Corkman now rates over 30,000 in print run per week. What has surprised me is how many people away from home receive a local paper from their families each week. They love anything anecdotal: analysis of a current situation or a recall about an event of the past. This amounts to a treasury of local history, putting on record what would otherwise be lost to memory. I often get letters from readers giving their reminiscences – matters for further research.

I am fortunate in that I particularly appreciate the resonance of words in common usage among the people with whom I live. I am partial to a direct style of writing. It now comes naturally once I have rounded out some idea. Very often that process of rounding out takes place through lateral thinking in the car or at night before I drop off to sleep. I keep a notebook by the bed to sketch out a sequence of thought. Otherwise you will rack your brain in the morning in the effort to remember! A few key phrases is all you need.

I do not have a photographic memory. Still, once I get the flow of a poem it will stay with me and may emerge into consciousness as the occasion requires. It is surely a spin-off from the practice of memorising, which was a feature of our schooling.

What I thank God for is a capability to associate ideas and fill out a context. It is a pattern of lateral thinking which brings different aspects of an idea into focus. One may picture it as emptying a washing machine. You pull out a sheet, and then shirts, pyjamas, towels and stockings follow on in the mix.

In school we were all expected to memorise poetry. It was not then perceived as an arbitrary imposition. It was taken quite for granted as part of education. It certainly has not been a burden over the years. Many of us can still come up with an apt quotation from Shakespeare as the occasion requires. Young people today do not have that rich background as they start out in life. Having it entered on a database in a computer is of little effect in comparison to having it inscribed on one's mind with all its emotional associations.

Those walks through the country with the dogs are lightened by snatches of Irish and English poetry learned by rote six decades ago in Meelin school. 'A violet by a mossy stone half hidden from the eye, fair as a star when only one is shining in the sky.' 'Ag gabháil an sléibhe dom trathnóna do labhair na heanlaithe liom go brónach, do labhair an naosg binn 's an crotach glórach ag faisnéis dom gur éag mo stórach.' In my memory that verse is as fresh as when I first learned it at school and shared that sense of nature being in harmony with the grief suffered by the poor woman who had lost her son.

– THE LOCAL RADIO INTEREST –

North Cork Local Radio had been operating as a 'pirate' radio station for a number of years when the possibility of obtaining a franchise as a licensed station came on stream. Up and down the country many such 'pirate' stations were setting out to regularise their positions. They were in most cases commercial operations backed by a small number of wealthy shareholders. The concept of a co-operative venture with a broad base of small shareholders proved particularly attractive. I readily responded to an invitation to join the committee and later to become chairman.

We knew that we had a mountain to climb; first to compete successfully for the licence, and second to put together a war chest to get on air and survive until the cash flow from advertising made ends meet. What we had on our side was an extraordinary measure of commitment on the ground. That applied to the pre-existing North Cork Local Radio with its multitude of small shareholders and to its established listenership. It applied particularly to the expanded Board of Management, especially to those with essential business experience and with technical skills. The morale reflected what one might expect to find in a highly motivated GAA team and its band of supporters when facing what others would see as insurmountable odds. The business people generously provided their time and expertise without expectation of any reward for their work. Even though it was a major personal demand, no one was prepared to let the side down by not giving of their best.

As regards the key professional personnel we had the good fortune to have on board Colm O'Conaill as chief executive and John Cahill as radio technician extraordinaire. Colm with experience in every aspect of radio had exceptional business talent. We could not have succeeded without him. John could set up a state-of-the-art electronic system in the studio and could commission a submarine generator from a British shipyard as stand-by in case of power failure at the mast. We were satisfied that we had the technical requirements in place and the key personnel to run the business of radio. The major challenge then was to secure the financial support required to fund the whole operation. We knew that without that in place our application for a licence would not be accepted by the Irish Radio and Television Commission (IRTC).

It was here that the support of the Diocese of Cloyne was crucial to the launch of the North Cork Community Radio, County Sound. Bishop John Magee authorised me to write around to the parishes requesting *pro rata* contributions. This brought in around £25,000. If there was ever seed capital this certainly was it. With that amount in hand we approached the Bank of Ireland for the requisite loan. A co-operative with a large number of small shareholders seeking a loan without the standard collateral is generally a non-starter at the desk in the bank manager's office. However, where the goodwill of all parishes in a diocese is at stake that puts a different complexion on matters. That counts as virtual collateral with the moguls at headquarters in Dublin.

In response to the grant of the requisite loan we made a commitment that if we obtained the franchise we would seek new shareholders on sums of £50 or multiples thereof. This would later require a tour of our North Cork catchment area. I then came to appreciate what life is like for a local politician out canvassing votes. With Donagh Murphy of Dromagh as companion we trekked around Duhallow Saturday after Saturday. Donagh knew everyone and could rate the quality of potential givers. The response was amazingly generous. People appreciated our commitment. The amounts collected in any day would range between £5,000 and £7,000. Sean Ryan, manager of the Bank of Ireland in Mallow, saw that his trust in us had not been misplaced. We owed it to ourselves as much as to him.

On 21 September 1989 we signed the contract for the broadcasting franchise with IRTC. On 26 January 1990 North Cork Community Radio Co-operative Society (NCCR), trading as County Sound 103.7 FM, went on air from its studio in Mallow. I expect that in passing that vote of confidence in us the IRTC must have felt that it was a gamble to release a small rural co-operative into a field where so many big players were competing. We gained a more secure position when IRTC approved the link-up between NCCR and Radio Cork Limited which had been trading poorly on its Cork City and County franchise. Consequently a separate joint venture company, trading as Radio County Sound Ltd, was established to manage and operate the licences of both companies. This also incorporated West Cork local radio based in Bandon.

Eventually on 30 August 2001 Radio County Media Ltd, of which Radio County Sound Ltd is a subsidiary, was acquired by UTV. The resultant link with a market leader in television, radio and print media has put Cork 96 and 103 FM in a strong position to compete into the future. The agreement signed between NCCR and Radio Cork Ltd on 9 September 1991 remains in place and NCCR is entitled to retain two directors on the board of Radio County Sound Ltd to secure its interest. It has been my privilege to have been chairman of that company over many years.

The above is an overview of the various structural steps experienced by our local radio through the years. The philosophy of local radio which was set out in our original mission statement has remained the dominating motivation. We have proved that a broad-based community radio is commercially viable when it effectively identifies the needs and interests of its target audience. This is how we saw the remit of County Sound 103 FM in terms of its community philosophy to which we were committed.

County Sound 103 FM should become a catalyst in promoting projects and developments which enhance the quality of life in its franchise area, be they educational, religious, cultural, environmental or economic. It should provide local charitable and benevolent organisations with the opportunity to explain their aims and to appeal for public support. It should have a special concern for those living in isolated areas with a view to keeping them in contact with local and national developments and to providing them with a sense of place by its coverage of community, cultural and sporting events.

Looking back over those fifteen years one accepts that it was a challenge, but a very worthwhile challenge. Working with so many talented people was a learning experience in working out strategies and tactics – and in taking momentous decisions on which the future of our radio depended. The original NCCR board members have down the years generously volunteered their time and energy as I did without expectation of material reward.

What I have found most fulfilling is presenting the religious programmes *Sunday Forum* and *Thought on Sunday*. Here one needs to identify the interests of one's audience and relate the Christian faith to their concerns. Later I undertook a variety programme around midday on Sunday. It works on an open agenda, commenting on anything and everything that comes the way. With a life-long background in country lore I discovered that here also was something which large numbers of the audience shared with me. There was not a day that someone would not stop me in the street to comment on some item or other which had been raised in those midday programmes. People seemed tired of the endless media discussion on bad news and sensational issues. Communing with nature has a healing effect and for older listeners in particular it would revive the memories of younger days. County Sound was here tapping into the interest shown in the documentaries presented by Gerrit Van Gelderen and Eamonn de Buitleir and of course the RTÉ Radio programme *Mooney Goes Wild on One*.

Those who bought shares in NCCR around the time of its launch saw them as free contributions. They did not regard them as investments into the future. It was then a great day when we found ourselves in a position to reward them at the handsome premium of €5.50 per £1 share. The sum for distribution of around €500,000 came from what NCCR received from the sale of its shareholding in 1996 in the course of the management buy-out at County Media Ltd. The position of County Sound 103.7 FM is well secured into the future by binding agreements with its parent company. There was little point in holding €500,000 on deposit indefinitely.

For myself, that twenty years as chairman of NCCR has been something of a roller-coaster ride. The IRTC must have been surprised when the small co-operative actually got on air. They must have been more surprised when it consolidated its position. Fortunately NCCR took opportunities as they offered through a number of strategic alliances. This policy has brought us to our current position of strength as part of a powerful coalition in the Irish media world when our parent company County Media Ltd was acquired by UTV on 30 August 2001. This has proved a great advantage towards guaranteeing our position into the future no matter what challenges that future may hold. The splendid new studios on Gouldshill speak for our success at this juncture in our history. If the board had not had the foresight and the courage to take those opportunities as they offered along the way NCCR, if it had survived at all, would have been just a small community radio depending totally on local advertising.

Back in 1996 after NCCR had cashed in its radio shareholding in the course of the management buy-out we discussed the future structure of NCCR. The most desirable option seemed to be the conversion of the co-operative into a voluntary society or association such as that which operates in the case of the Friends of Mallow Hospital. North Cork Community Radio would continue to relate to County Sound Ltd precisely as NCCR had always related in preserving its particular ethos and interest.

One thing that I learned from the NCCR experience was the need to think constructively and imaginatively. I see this quality as something which we Churchmen often lack. 'Thinking outside the box' is not our forte. For the launch of Millennium 2000, NCCR proposed that it fund a major celebration in St Colman's Cathedral in Cobh. This with the title 'Voices of Cloyne' would have incorporated all the choirs in the Diocese to highlight a dramatic presentation of the different phases in the history of the Church in Ireland since the coming of St Patrick. The sequence was the brain-child of the Duhallow Choir under its gifted director Donal O'Callaghan. The choirs were already rehearsing and NCCR had drawn up its detailed plans for amplification and lighting. Unhappily it all fell through. It would have required more human resources than were available at the time. What a spiritual experience it would have been in that beautiful setting of our glorious Cathedral! The promised video would have shown it at its best. Without being too parochial it would have surpassed the Millennium Experience staged by the Diocese of Kerry in Millstreet's Green Glens Arena, impressive as that certainly was. Perhaps we will have another opportunity when the work on the Cathedral is completed.

CHAPTER 5

MINISTRY IN THE DIOCESE

During my half century as a priest there have been just two bishops of the Diocese of Cloyne: Bishop John Ahern, from 1956 to 1986, and Bishop John Magee, ordained in 1987. In them we have seen two quite different personalities. Inevitably both have also been men and bishops of their times – and those times could hardly have been more dissimilar.

A straw in that wind of change was the manner of address when one spoke to a bishop. For Bishop Ahern the style of address was typically 'My Lord'. For Bishop Magee from the very start it was 'Bishop John'. Personally I am happy with that. It is respectfully friendly without being overly familiar. Bishop Ahern as Professor in Maynooth had taught me canon law. The class textbook was the 1918 *Code*. That comprehensive text left little space for improvisation and little for any show of original thinking. As I have mentioned already the 1918 *Code* had stereotyped the compass of the canon law. It was only later in the Dunboyne Institute when we heard the critique of the pre-*Code* canonist Dr Ned O'Brien, then Parish Priest of Clondalkin in Dublin, that we students appreciated that crucial point. Ned O'Brien lamented the way in which the 1918 *Code* had confined canon law in a straitjacket, leaving little space for discretion and equity. He would spell out an anomaly. Equity had been introduced into the English common law tradition from the old principles of canon law by Lord Chancellors who were traditionally Churchmen. It was a profoundly Christian concept. Now that same equity had lost out to the cold letter of the law in the 1918 *Code*. He would pronounce that the letter kills but the spirit gives life.

In the event Dr Ahern had little opportunity to show his undoubted intelligence. I learned afterwards how he had been a star performer right through his studies. Perhaps we should have tested him more when we had the opportunity at that later post-graduate level in Dunboyne House. He was totally at home in the academic life of Maynooth. He certainly did not welcome the call to become Bishop of Cloyne. His friends in Maynooth later told me that he had assumed the office out of pure obedience to the will of the Holy Father. I believe that. It was surely the spirit in which he lived the ministry of bishop. From the very start his episcopal colleagues had held him in the highest regard. They trusted his understanding of complex issues and they prized his wisdom in dealing with human situations. Even when he had retired to Nazareth House in Mallow they would consult with him constantly.

It was in Nazareth House that I came to know him best. Now retired with the burden of episcopacy off his shoulders he could think and speak as a free man. It was a pleasure to call on him and there raise questions of every kind. Many a time a question would be mischievously aired to add heat to his response. *Mea culpa*! His knowledge was encyclopaedic. The history of Ireland; the history of the Diocese of Cloyne; the history of the Second Vatican Council: you name it and he showed himself master. It was then that I appreciated what his Maynooth colleagues had said about his outstanding intelligence. Not only had he total recall of the relevant hard facts, but he could also analyse various points of view. His motto might have been 'facts are sacred, opinions are free', but on that opinion score one never got a free passage! Every angle would be subjected to challenge and scrutiny.

But John Ahern was inherently a painfully reserved person when it came to revealing his mind in public. Among friends in private one knew where he stood on any and every question.

Let a journalist of any hue appear on the horizon and that was that. All of us who knew him felt that it would be a shame if he carried to the grave what he knew on so many fronts. Here I am referring to more than his memories of the past. Even more valuable was his constant updating of his views. He was the old style polymath, a voracious reader and a highly critical one at that. Everything was grist to the mill. To him applied that oft quoted saying of an ancient Roman dramatist: *Homo sum, humani nil a me alienum puto* (All humanity interests me as a man).

Anyway I believed that I had a duty to posterity to get him to speak on the record. Two of his close friends put it to me strongly. But how to short-circuit his reservations! I contacted the County Sound technician John Cahill who was expert on all forms of modern technology in the radio business. On his advice I sourced a highly sensitive multi-directional recording microphone. Armed discreetly with this I called out to Nazareth House. As I guided the conversation out of familiar territory he eventually smelled a rat. I admitted that my intention was to have him on record and then submit the finished product for his judgement. Strangely enough, I think that he genuinely regretted deep inside that the operation had not succeeded. We others certainly did regret it.

Bishop John Ahern presented as stern and humourless. Yet when someone came to him in any distress he was kindness itself and took a genuinely personal interest in their case. As for humour he loved a good session when the jokes flowed. He enjoyed repartee and always took with good grace the quick riposte to some comment of his. I recall two incidents of this in my own experience.

One was at my very first Confirmation ceremony in Mallow when a persistent pain in the neck (literally!) had made him impatient with us priests. In the sacristy afterward he gave voice to his grievances. He turned to me, who was taking matters lightly, and snapped: 'What's more, you forgot to incense me at the Offertory.' 'Well my Lord,' I said, 'I felt you were incensed enough'! He greeted this with the hint of a smile and remarked: 'Well, didn't I ask for that!'

On another occasion a group of us priests were with him at the church gate in Kildorrery when that lively family of O'Callaghan children in a passing car recognised me from Maynooth days. The mother, an Italian at one remove, made straight for me with her usual *abbracio*. As she left some of the group looked at the Bishop expectantly. 'Well, Denis,' he said, 'wasn't she a bit over familiar?' I noted the glint in his eye and said: 'My Lord Bishop, it's not the women who kiss your priests in public you should be watching.' Again that hint of a smile and shake of the head.

John Ahern's programme of life in Nazareth House was predictable. It was punctuated by his spiritual exercises through the day beginning with Morning Prayer and Mass at 8.30 a.m. The nine o'clock news and weather saw him ready to retire. All his usual visitors knew his style. It so happened that on the evening of his death I had fished for some sea trout for his lunch on the morrow. Time ran late – any angler will appreciate how this may happen! As I came in the door home just after the nine o'clock news the telephone rang from Nazareth House to say that Bishop Ahern had just died. I naturally regretted that but for my delay on the river bank I would have been there with him. Given his devotion to St Joseph I know that he did not die alone.

Now with John Ahern the man out of the way we can turn to John Ahern the bishop. When he was appointed, the template for the life and work of an Irish bishop had been consolidated over generations. One really did then step into the shoes of one's predecessor. Donning the mitre set the protocol for the characteristic episcopal role in the years before the Second Vatican Council. In the previous century there would have been dominant figures like Cardinal Paul Cullen of Dublin and Archbishop John McHale of Tuam. They had certainly ploughed individual furrows but by Bishop Ahern's time there was a clearly marked beaten path. Anyone tempted to diverge from that path would be aware of strong personalities like Archbishop John Charles McQuaid of Dublin and Bishop Michael Brown of Galway looking disapprovingly over one's shoulder.

If Bishop Ahern was anything as bishop he was 'a safe pair of hands'. In fact that description would come readily to his lips when he passed favourable judgement on some solid predictable ecclesiastic. He endorsed discretion as cardinal virtue. Anyone who transgressed his criterion would be branded a loose mouth or a loose cannon. Prudence for him was definitely the better part of valour. In fact there was the danger that prudence could operate as cannibal virtue, leaving little space for the positive pastoral aspects of that same virtue in the teaching of St Thomas Aquinas.

He would say that his mind did not operate well on a white page and so I would frequently be commissioned to provide a draft for him on some item or other. Once he had a text in front of him it would prime his critical talent into action. Priests were all too aware of this trait of his when they submitted particulars on some project. The term coined was 'snaghunting'. One wag who was expert in legal Latin slogans invoked the proverb *Bonum ex integra causa, malum ex quocumque defecto*. A case only passes muster if it qualifies on all counts. A single fault vitiates the lot.

The result was that he certainly maintained the diocese on even keel. Financially it remained always in a very strong position. Any project which involved a draw on central fund would be carefully scrutinised. When he issued a long-term loan to a parish for major church restoration it was with some reluctance. He was convinced that the commitment of parishioners to restoring their parish church should remain their priority. He appreciated that if this duty was taken from them they would be most unlikely to respond to other calls for support.

This trait of good housekeeping had its downside. In a way it reflected his own character. His living conditions were spartan. His personal spending was minimal. There was certainly need for more capital investment by parishes, particularly after the Second Vatican Council had raised the sights on pastoral care. One now regrets that so many town parishes did not secure accommodation for parish centres when such was readily available. The feeling was that the bishop would see those as surplus to requirements.

No Irish bishop had followed the deliberations at the Second Vatican Council so intently as had Bishop John Ahern. The ideas both enlightened and inspired him. He understood deep inside the pastoral challenges for Ireland in the years ahead. If he had been a man of action in the right environment this would have been a golden opportunity.

As I have explained above, the questions raised and the recommendations made at the Council had caught us in Ireland unawares. After the Council we certainly set up a representative panel of commissions but in the absence of commitment to put in place an overall pastoral strategy those agencies led a fragmented existence on the margins. The well-tried system of the past continued. We now see that the parable of new wine/new bottles had a lesson for us. We did not appreciate the urgency.

I trust that I have drawn a balanced picture of Bishop John Ahern, someone for whom I have had the greatest respect. He was single minded in his commitment to being true to the Lord in his vocation as priest and bishop. In all regards he was a man of his time. For my part I could not have had more support than what he provided for any worthwhile ideas put to him during my years in the parish of Mallow. Not that he would be slow to raise questions but his advice was invariably sound. 'Ah well,' he would finally say, 'sure 'tis up to yourself. I won't stand in your way.' From him this was approval enough.

– A NEW BISHOP –

After it became known that the resignation proffered by Bishop John Ahern had been accepted by Pope John Paul II, speculation about likely successors continued apace. The Nuncio would have sent around the standard confidential circular seeking information on suitable candidates. In former times the diocesan clergy would have voted on a *terna*, a panel of their three candidates to be forwarded to the Vatican. In more recent years the influence of the diocesan clergy has become quite secondary. Now individual negative reports have a more marked influence than any positive recommendations. That leaves the field quite open for a surprise appointment.

This was our experience when the name of Monsignor John Magee was announced as the new Bishop of Cloyne. I would have known him as a student at the Irish College in Rome in the early sixties and in his role beside Pope John Paul II on his visit to Maynooth in 1979. Everyone quickly learned of his days as secretary to the three popes – Paul VI, John Paul I and John Paul II. What recommended him to me in particular was that he was a member of the Kiltegan Fathers who are committed to missionary work in Nigeria. Father John Magee had been a member of their team in that challenging field.

I had been frequently making the case that more Irish bishops should come from our religious and missionary outreach. After all Ireland had produced vast numbers of such priests from whom one could name at least four Irish priests who were then or had been Superior Generals of international orders and congregations. Surely they would have a vast amount of pastoral experience on which to draw as Ireland faced new challenges at home, challenges which churches in other parts of the globe had already been called on to meet on the ground.

I can only guess at the mixed feelings with which members of the episcopal bench greeted the appointment of Bishop John Magee. It must have been as big a surprise to most of them as to us. I suppose they would have perceived his stay in Cloyne as of temporary duration before he would be called on to serve the Church in further fields. That would also have been the perception in Cloyne itself. For us meantime we looked forward to new ideas and initiatives on the pastoral front once the bishop had become acquainted with the needs and resources of the diocese.

It was surely a major change for him, from the very heart of the Church in Rome to its margins in Cloyne. We certainly did not expect him to hit the ground running. There has never been a question about Bishop Magee's capacity for hard work. As secretary to three popes, administration would have come as second nature to him. Taking decisions in which finality was called for from him would have been a challenge, particularly in a new field of operations. Here he always consulted until he had built up experience on the ground – even then he would look for advice on all the angles. If problems emerged later he would never shift blame to the advisers. That was a quality of the man which we admired.

The first challenge which confronted the new bishop was that of rectifying the age profile of priests in the diocese. Bishop Ahern had certainly shied away from addressing that sensitive issue of disturbing a comfort zone. Many parish priests had well exceeded the seventy-five-year high water mark when by the canon law now in force they should have submitted to the bishop their resignation from office. The age profile of the priests in the diocese was certainly out of balance. Fr Robert Forde, one of our Mallow team of priests, quipped that he rated for the Guinness Book of Records as the oldest serving curate in Christendom!

Everyone was watching the new bishop on this first trial for testing his mettle. It was expected that the long-serving cohort who had borne the burden of the day and the heat would stand fast in the showdown and would gain a stay of execution. However, the bishop held the high political ground with Monsignor Dan O'Connell of Macroom, whom he had confirmed in the role of Vicar General. Monsignor Dan, affectionately known as 'the Soldier' from his army chaplaincy days, was held in high regard by his contemporaries. Once he opted to submit his resignation as Parish Priest of Macroom the precedent had been set and the rest followed.

If Monsignor Dan had not made that first move so readily matters might not have gone that smoothly. Some were mentioning questions raised in the Archdiocese of Dublin about retroactivity of canon law and whether the dispensation in the new *Code* could affect the position of parish priests originally appointed without any restriction in regard to duration of service. It was recalled also that a parish priest well into his eighties in a neighbouring diocese had kept a newly appointed bishop at bay by feigning lack of appreciation of the bishop's reminder about retirement at age seventy-five. The priest, when he finally got the message, closed his ear trumpet with a flourish and declared contentedly 'Of course, my Lord. But sure I am well beyond that age now'! He had traversed the reef and was now in a lagoon.

– WORKING IN PARTNERSHIP –

Bishop John Magee appointed me to the office of Vicar General. Under canon law this qualifies one as Local Ordinary with jurisdiction across the diocese. In that role I and the other Vicar General, Monsignor Jim O'Donnell of Macroom, worked very closely with Bishop Magee in the work of the diocese. I think that we were a well-balanced team. I would usually be for forging ahead once the case seemed solid whereas Jim would present second thoughts on the possible downside. Perhaps I would read human nature through rose-tinted glasses whereas Jim would remind us of Murphy's Law to the effect that whatever can go wrong will go wrong. And at the worst possible time.

The bishop would listen so as to get a fix on the overall situation and a consensus would generally emerge. He appreciated honest speaking of one's mind up front. I suppose this is a feature of life today as against the bogus expressions of agreement in days gone by. One then preserved one's personal reservations until the bishop was out of earshot. It was said that when one was appointed a bishop one could rest secure in the knowledge that one would never lack for a square meal and that one would never again be told the truth!

One of the most sensitive areas in diocesan organisation is that of appointing personnel in the various parishes. Sometimes one would hear that a particular priest was not suited to or not happy in a position. That might result from tension between priests themselves or between priest and people. Human nature being human nature, even in the ordained ministry, all kinds of situation do arise. It is a priority not to stand by and allow some such situation to fester.

From the beginning Bishop Magee put down a marker to the effect that it was the pastoral requirements of a given ministry that would prove decisive in making an appointment. This was a valuable corrective to the former understanding that ministries should be assessed as promotional posts. In addition a term of six years or so now came to be accepted as the ordinary duration of appointments, apart from those of parish priests. Indeed, the *Code of Canon Law* now authorises the bishop to appoint parish priests for a limited duration. This has not yet been implemented in our diocese.

Bishop Magee always consults with individual priests when appointments are proposed. Our consultative group will have added our insights. He listens to the various pastoral and human concerns so that every situation may then be assessed in the round. The result is that when appointments are made priests are as a rule content with the decisions in the knowledge that they have been dealt with fairly and sensitively. It is true to say that in any walk of life being prepared to accept decisions made without prejudice tends to work out better for oneself as well. There is the story about the lone parish priest, a thorny character by nature, who badgered his bishop to give him an assistant. The bishop identified a candidate of strong character who would not be browbeaten. Later the parish priest confided in a friend that there was one thing worse than not having a curate and that was having a curate!

For the ongoing administration of the diocese there were standing councils and committees with particular remits. One of the most representative was the Council of Priests with a broad membership drawn principally from priests across the diocese. Bishop Magee chaired this council in its earlier years. Later the chairman was selected from among the members. Canon law identified the Council of Priests as the Bishop's Senate to advise on the broad spectrum of pastoral life in the diocese. There is the risk that a Council of Priests may tend to focus on the concerns of priests and so become a Council for Priests. This is an occupational hazard where the priest members select their chairman with a view to meeting their concerns. In our case the counterpoise is having the bishop to direct and approve the agenda in advance of meetings.

In our case we went through the growing pains of dealing with the personal concerns of the priests. With that out of the way the broader pastoral needs of the diocese have moved centre stage. Some of these needs were administrative, such as the establishment of parish pastoral councils. The others more immediately pastoral were the establishing of structures on the ground for more effective evangelisation in the contemporary culture. Here liturgy and catechesis are still as ever primary concerns. However, in circumstances of today those concerns took on a different shape. Unless pastoral structures and approaches addressed these circumstances they would be stillborn. That is where the Council of Priests becomes most relevant. With its broad representation it should bring valuable experience to bear on identifying pastoral priorities and on evaluating particular projects in the expanding field of evangelisation.

This was certainly a learning curve for us in a diocese which had essentially remained traditional and conservative right through and after the Vatican Council. I have already spoken of how influential the French pastoral experience had been at that Council. In the very secularised, broadly anti-clerical world which had emerged in France the Catholic Church early in the 1900s had come to recognise the country as 'missionary territory'. *France, pays de mission* was the title of a well-known book by Abbé Michoneau in my student days. This was a theme which the far-seeing Canon JG McGarry, founder of *The Furrow*, had addressed with us in Maynooth in the fifties. We thought that he was over-the-top when he directed that we in Ireland should watch this space. How right he was!

Bishop Magee was given to quoting a saying of Pope John Paul II to the effect that every new generation is a fresh territory to be won for Christ. This was never more true than it is today in view of the pace of change. The bishop took up this theme at Millennium 2000 when he addressed his personal mission statement as Bishop of Cloyne to both the College of Consultors and the Council of Priests. It was something on which he had evidently spent quality time in reflection and prayer during retreat. As he communicated it to us one could see that he spoke from the heart. It was really inspiring as the expression of his commitment as bishop to serve the call of the Gospel at this time. The question was whether we could measure up to speed on this missionary pilgrimage. The days of staying with the pace of the slower camels were still casting shadows over our onward progress.

The reality of still having an unusually large number of priests serving in the diocese has proved to be a mixed blessing for Cloyne. In this regard other neighbouring dioceses are perceived to be moving into crisis management as numbers fall. In the Diocese of Killaloe parishes are being clustered and parish pastoral councils are being entrusted with greater authority and responsibility for organising the day-to-day life of parishes. This system has been brought into being with little enough time for preparation on the ground. What is most impressive is the readiness and competence of lay people to shoulder the responsibility. Naturally there are bound to be growing pains but already the general level of collaboration between priests and people is exemplary.

We in Cloyne were fortunate in that with our relatively high number of priests we had the time to develop similar structures for that collaboration and we learn from the experience of the pilot schemes which now operate in other dioceses. Basic structures are already being put in place here. We instance parish pastoral councils and parish finance councils. It is in the latter that parishioners have taken a lot of burdensome work from priests. When it comes to assessing plans for capital works in the parish lay people are well qualified. Similarly there are always people on hand to audit the parish accounts and to advise on investments. Very few priests are now left with the fruitless and time-wasting chore of counting the money taken in on the weekly collections. Trusted and well-resourced parish pastoral councils are now a priority. Identifying a team of committed and well-experienced personnel is a major challenge.

Much of a priest's time is currently taken up with the schools in the parish. Traditionally the priest acted in the role of manager and whatever had to be done was landed on him. Now as chairman of the Board of Management he tends to remain still more or less in that same traditional role. This is fast changing with professional and competent lay members serving on the board. They are ready to place their business and personal expertise in administration at the service of the board. True, there was concern that parents on boards would restrict their interests to shorter-term issues which would be of benefit to the current cohort of pupils. However, with more professional attitudes now commonplace and with a greater sense of ownership of the school this concern has corrected itself.

Of course, there is one outstanding pastoral concern in the minds of many priests: the concern for the catechesis of children. We have explained above how our national school system has developed so as to encompass the positive role of teachers in communicating the faith to the children. There are certain to be major changes in that tradition within the foreseeable future. We priests will then find ourselves organising an alternative system for the catechesis of younger children and for the religious education of older students. Here close collaboration between teachers and parents will be essential. Indeed, we already see the first steps towards that collaboration in the catechetical programme for First Eucharist *Do This in Memory*. Here the priest feels more at home in the pastoral scene where he should be rather than in day-to-day school administration. Most important is the sense of partnership with parents and teachers.

Into the future we will see more adolescents and more young adults who have not been baptised. Some proportion of these will come from Catholic homes where the duty of christening young children has not been addressed. An increasing number will come from immigrant families who wish to become members of the Catholic Church. The Rite for the Christian Initiation of Adults (RCIA) is now in place in Ireland generally. This is quite new for us. The process of initiating catechumens into the local Christian community would have had a long tradition in Irish missionary territories where catechists had a central role to play. That process would also have been standard in the early Church where the conversion of adults would have been the norm. The revised programme which is now in place here is well adapted to the developing culture of faith in Ireland.

– Developing a Church Culture –

In the Second Vatican Council the concept of the Church as primarily a community came to the fore. There is nothing novel about the concept. It was already taught in so many words by St Paul. 'You are Christ's body, organs of it depending on one another' (1 Corinthians 12:27). This Church/Communion approach put that of Church/Society in the correct perspective. The German sociological terms *Gemeinschaft* and *Gesellschaft* sum up the interplay of the twin concepts. The society (*Gesellschaft*) is to be at the service of the community (*Gemeinschaft*). The standard textbooks which we students had followed in our theological study of the Church had centred attention on the hierarchical society. Perhaps here also the *Code of Canon Law* had cast a strong shadow as it set out in detail that structural framework of Church/Society.

This shadow had not been dispelled by the formal teaching of Pius XII in his encyclical letter *Mystici Corporis* of 1943. There he had brought centre stage the traditional scriptural concept of the Church as Communion, the unity of Christians with Christ and with each other, within a Church which is both hidden mystery and visible society. That visible society is to reflect and promote the hidden mystery of salvation in Christ the Saviour. This was already taught in the schema *De Ecclesia* of the First Vatican Council (1870):

> Such is the admirable representation of the Church which should be set before the minds of the faithful, so that it may be firmly anchored there, and which cannot be over-stressed; the head of the Church is Christ; it is from him that the whole body, firmly held together and united by an operation proportionate to each member, derives its growth in order to be built up in charity.

In our student days in Maynooth that understanding of the Church as Communion was seen more as material for spiritual formation than for dogmatic theology. It remained on the margins even though in the postgraduate school we had been made aware of the salient principles in the abstract. For me the moment of truth came when I discovered a book by the French Dominican Jerome Hamer. The original 1962 French edition appeared in English in 1964 under the title *The Church is a*

Communion. Once I began to read it I burned the midnight oil. It has remained one of my favourite books in pastoral theology. When I read it again recently on retreat it endorsed the first impression. It blends the teaching of Scripture into the theological tradition which has now culminated in *Lumen gentium* of the Second Vatican Council.

That Dogmatic Constitution on the Church has been accepted as the crowning glory of Vatican II. I will not attempt to provide a summary here of the depth and wealth of its teaching. Chapter II on the Church as the new People of God is central to underpinning the pastoral mission of the Council. 'People of God' refers to the whole community of the Church, encompassing all the faithful, lay and ordained. There are a variety of ministries all working together for the good of the whole body. All share each in their own ways in the priestly, prophetic and kingly functions of Christ the Saviour.

What was said in the Council has been the blueprint for the theology of the lay faithful in all Church teaching since. Collaboration is the key to achieving here on earth the kingdom for which Christians pray in the Our Father. This is put very gently in the chapter on the Laity in *Lumen gentium*:

> Their sacred pastors know how much the laity contribute to the welfare of the whole Church. Pastors also know that they themselves were not meant to shoulder alone the entire saving mission of the Church towards the world. On the contrary, they understand that it is their noble duty so to shepherd the faithful and recognise their services and charismatic gifts that all according to their proper roles may cooperate in this common undertaking with one heart. (par. 30)

Even though Jerome Hamer's book was published while Vatican II was in preparation it is still to my mind essential reading. Indeed his theology may be more relevant than might appear at first sight. Not only is it redolent of that rich French tradition in pastoral theology but over the years its author has worked closely with Cardinal Joseph Ratzinger as consultant in the Congregation for the Doctrine of the Faith.

However, better than any written theological guidelines is to see lay people sharing in ministry. Already we have made progress in Ireland on the integration of the laity into parish liturgy and parish administration. All parishes have now appointed Ministers of the Word and Ministers of the Eucharist. Lay people have found roles in Church administration as members of pastoral and finance councils. Even more important in the ministry of evangelisation is the traditional work of our teachers in the handing on of the faith and in the formation of children for the reception of the Sacraments. They are lay ministers *par excellence*.

The next step continues to be problematic where it impinges on clerical status and identity. We are comfortable with lay people being given roles in the parish where these roles are in the gift of the priest and so affirm his position and identity. This does not amount to that true collaboration where lay members operate as part of a team in mutual recognition and respect. At the washing of the feet in the Gospel of St John, Jesus accepts that he is truly Teacher and Master but that his ministry is at the service of others. There surely is an important message for us priests on how to exercise our pastoral ministry. Again it is principally a matter of attitude as to how far we are prepared to share responsibility and authority.

Thirty or so years ago a traditionally minded priest spoke at a deanery conference in Dublin about the ministry of the lay person. He quoted with approval the comments of a Presbyterian minister who had cautioned him against allowing too much scope to lay people in the running of Church affairs. His experience of the role played by the Select Vestry had not been a happy one. The speaker went on from there to cite Vatican II on the secular mission of the laity. He quoted the texts which call on the laity to make the Gospel present and operative in the world where they are and to act as the salt of the earth. This for him concluded the mission of the laity.

It is true that in Vatican II we read: 'The laity by their vocation seek the Kingdom of God by engaging in temporal affairs and by ordering them according to the plan of God. They live in the world, that is, in each and in all of the secular professions and occupations' (*On the Church* par. 31). That is not the full balanced picture of lay ministry. It is just one key aspect of it. In that same constitution on the Church there is much stress on the ministry of the laity as working in collaboration with the ordained ministry: 'Let every opportunity be given them so that, according to their abilities and the needs of the times, they may zealously participate in the saving work of the Church' (par. 33).

In travels around the world I have observed some very positive models of collaborative ministry. I have spoken already about Fr Eugene O'Sullivan of Auckland and the community which gathered in his chaplaincy centre. He is one of many others in New Zealand. In Australia I got to know very well Fr John McSweeney, native of Inchageela and now retired parish priest of an urban parish in Kingsgrove in Sydney. He had working with him a team of lay people, both volunteers and salaried. It was a joy to see them so committed and so united in the ministry. Morale was high because they had that common sense of mission in which each had a role to play. The respect they showed to and for each other was a striking witness. I identify these two Irish priests as good models of collaborative ministry. It has been claimed that in times past priests ordained from here for dioceses in the English-speaking world would have brought with them the strong clericalist character of our culture. They would have tended to see their role uncritically as an outreach of the Irish Church experience.

We see anti-clericalism as a negative factor in Irish society. We must also be concerned about clericalism. In dealing with this we still have a distance to go. Without question dioceses and parishes will soon see the necessity of adding qualified lay people to their pastoral teams. This will happen finally because of crisis due to shortage of priests. It should happen earlier because of our genuine appreciation that lay people are entitled to be admitted to minister in their particular roles for promoting the Christian faith. Otherwise we are saying that the only true vocation to ministry is that of the ordained ministry and the religious!

I doubt that anyone would subscribe to that view in principle. If we clergy were to subscribe to it in practice then we would indeed continue to have serious questions to answer. The test on where heart and mind really stand on this basic issue is to ask whether we treat lay people as colleagues in ministry just as we treat our fellow priests. It comes down to that attitude of mutual respect.

It is true that diocese and parish will need to accept as a matter of justice that lay people in ministry be properly remunerated. We need to look to priorities if we are prepared to expend very large sums without question on bricks and mortar building projects and cavil about remunerating those committed to the pastoral ministry. The proper benchmarking level here for full-time qualified personnel may best be linked to the going rate for teachers. As someone who has been engaged for most of my life in the formation of priests it will be humbling to accept that many lay people may be better qualified than we priests are for the role of managing and directing strategic pastoral programmes. The ideal is team spirit. This summarises well what St Paul teaches at length in his letter to the Church in Corinth, which was riven with internal disagreements: 'Now there are varieties of gifts, but the same Spirit; and there are varieties of service, but the same Lord; and there are varieties of working, but it is the same God who inspires them all' (1 Corinthians 12:4-5). The witness of the Gospel requires that all be seen as working to establish the same kingdom. This must surely be inspired by a conviction of faith rather than by the pressure of necessity.

– REORDERING THE CATHEDRAL –

St Colman's Cathedral in Cobh is universally admired for its superb site and majestic beauty. In the language of estate agents, location, location, location determines to a large extent the material value of an ordinary dwelling house. How much more should its chosen site convey the spiritual impact of a Mother House which is called on to embrace the family of the faithful across a diocese and direct their minds to God. A number of Irish cathedrals do occupy commanding sites but none has a presence to equal that of St Colman's in Cobh. If ever a cathedral site were to possess a *genius loci* St Colman's certainly qualifies on this count.

To develop that site on its sloping shale terrain was a major undertaking of structural engineering. To carry the weight of the building there is as much stone embedded in the foundations as is in evidence in the actual edifice. The structural engineers did their work well in stabilising those same foundations. There is no sign of settlement after almost a century. The beautiful building was completed in 1915 at a cost of £235,000.

One may wonder why in view of that existing problem in developing the site some more convenient location had not been selected. The choice of site is said to have been due to a wish to stay with the location of the pre-existing parish church of Cobh. However, one would think that the choice of location for the cathedral, as earlier for that of the parish church, was determined by the inspiring presence which the site offered. To appreciate the cathedral at its most glorious one should view it from well out in the harbour. One is doubly fortunate if the recently restored carillon of forty-nine bells is ringing out the Angelus chimes with the perfect acoustics provided by a calm sea. On visits to the prison school on Spike Island with the Co. Cork VEC the return journey to Cobh was an experience in all weathers. With the cathedral bathed in sunlight the prospect on the way back was unforgettable. One imagines how this must have inspired the original master architects to erect a church worthy of that glorious location. In this they certainly measured up to all that the natural potential offered. On the quality of the building itself I recall how at every opportunity the sculptor Seamus Murphy would visit Cobh to admire the stonework. This he recounts in his book *Stone Mad*. At the time he was an apprentice stoneworker in the limestone quarries in Meelin.

As today we cast eyes over the panorama stretching across the harbour out to the broad sweep of the Atlantic, the memory of sad times past throbs in us with a poignancy so well expressed long ago by the poet Virgil in his *Aeneid* as he reflects on the ups and downs of life in heroic times. *Sunt lacrimae rerum et mentem mortalia tangunt.* Here in truth for us too sorrow plucks at the heart and a sense of the transience of life weighs on the mind. The sadness now is in the thought of those innumerable thousands who had gathered into Queenstown, as Cobh was then known, with their minds set on emigration to the New World. Their hearts would have remained nostalgically back in their homes in the south of Ireland. Many bitter tears had flowed during the partings at the American wakes but there were still some tears left to shed as the last sight of land faded from view. Once the spire of the cathedral had been completed this would have remained the final memory of emigrants of a later age. The peal of the carillon would have sounded a sad farewell.

As one stands outside the door of the cathedral today and takes in that glorious panorama out to sea one should not forget that closer in down at your feet is the rail head, now housing the heritage centre, from which those thousands of Irish men, women and children had set their eyes on a new life far away from Ireland. Their story is well portrayed in the bronze sculpture on the quayside. In that superb sculpture of Annie Moore and her two little brothers the artist Jeanne Rynhart has captured the hopes of the many emigrants who stood on the wharf at Cobh. The families of those emigrants at home and abroad were the ones who had generously contributed to the building of our cathedral. It is for us a sacred trust to preserve and enhance that heritage as a monument to the living faith of the Irish then and now.

The Steering Committee established to plan and direct the work of restoration and reordering were very conscious of the responsibility laid upon them by Bishop Magee and the Diocese of Cloyne. They were also aware that the cathedral had been universally acclaimed as a gem of Gothic church architecture. So whatever was done would be subject to public scrutiny right across Ireland and beyond. After preliminary consultation Bishop Magee presented a formal brief for the consideration of a broadly representative briefing committee. This brief set out the overall parameters on the requirements for the celebration of liturgy in the cathedral. Vatican II regards the bishop as the chief steward of the mysteries of God. He is to act as governor, promoter and guardian of the entire liturgical life of the church committed to his care. It was with this remit in mind that Bishop Magee drafted the brief. It is essential background for anyone who wishes to appreciate the why and the wherefore of the proposed reordering. Bishop Magee was well qualified for the task due to his expertise in liturgy and his familiarity with inspired reorderings in cathedral churches across the world.

The Steering Committee, under its chairman Dr Tom Cavanagh of Fermoy, was a group of priests and lay personnel with a spectrum of expertise on all relevant aspects. Fr Denis Reidy, then the administrator of the parish of Cobh, was entrusted with the general remit of managing the enterprise on the ground. He proved the ideal choice to direct and oversee the progress of the work from first to last. Even though it was evident that the restoration would be a costly undertaking there was relief that the overall structures of the building including the roof timbers had well survived the years. The long exposure to severe weather and driving salt-laden air had indeed taken its toll on the surface mantle. The re-slating of the roof and the pointing of all the stone of the main building and spire were major undertakings. Once the areas of water ingress had been made good an underfloor heating system was then installed and the internal surfaces restored to their pristine condition. All that internal work will be really appreciated when an upgraded lighting system is in place.

The concern was that nothing should be spared in the quality of material and in the standard of work to leave the cathedral worthy of its original inspired builders. One can only wonder at the generosity of those past generations in providing funds for the building at a time when the Catholic population at home was impoverished. The cost of work at this date of writing on the conservation and preservation of the fabric has amounted to around €4million. The parish of Cobh and the parishes throughout the diocese are justifiably proud of what has been achieved to date. The grant of the European Heritage Award has put a seal on the excellence of the work.

What now remained to be addressed was the sensitive area of reordering the sanctuary to meet current requirements in keeping with the celebration of the liturgy as envisaged by the Second Vatican Council. In the original sanctuary the high altar with its tabernacle, reredos, screens and chapter stalls ranged around the *cathedra* of the bishop were all of one piece. It was evident that meeting the liturgical vision of Vatican II for active participation by the congregation around the altar could and should preserve that unity of the original sanctuary. That left the challenge of creating a design plan that would respect both the heritage and liturgy requirements.

I was privileged to have been entrusted with the role of chairing the specialist group which would recommend an architect for the work. I have served on many working groups over the years but none was as challenging and rewarding as this. The process of selecting an architect was certainly an awesome challenge. A sensitive and imaginative approach in terms of both the heritage and liturgy concerns was of the essence. To transfer a metaphor from the Socratic Method, the architect should read and deduce the model of a plan for liturgical reordering from the existing matrix. The various project plans submitted by a number of leading architects were certainly impressive in their different approaches to meeting the challenge. After a lot of heart searching it was the approach of Professor Cathal O'Neill that best recommended itself.

After the selection of architect had been endorsed by the Steering Committee the process of fleshing out the concepts and working through the details took a number of months during which a series of drafts was subjected to intensive scrutiny. The end result to my mind was superb, an ideal solution in keeping with the character of the cathedral. As the design plan for the extension to the sanctuary reached forward at a lower level it brought the congregation closer to the altar while providing an unobstructed view of the original sanctuary as inspiring background. One could just picture what imaginative lighting would have done for that.

Eventually the design came before An Bord Pleanála for planning permission. I attended the oral hearing of the case and remained convinced that the verdict could not be other than positive. The plan prepared by Professor Cathal O'Neill and his team represented an elegant solution to the challenge of blending the liturgical and heritage concerns. I fail to understand the rationale for the eventual refusal by the Board, particularly in view of the report that the design would have carried the recommendation of the chief planning officer, who had personally conducted the hearing. Our expectation of a positive outcome was bolstered by the architectural guidelines issued in 2003 by the Department of the Environment following on the Planning and Development Act 2002. Those guidelines from the Department had been accepted by the four main Christian churches in Ireland. The guidelines expressly called for a balance between the liturgical requirements and the architectural heritage of a listed church building, to the effect that the planning authorities should respect those requirements.

On analysis of the probable rationale behind the decision of An Bord Pleanála one concludes that while the Board formally accepted the need to give recognition to liturgical requirements, as they were obliged to do, they were not prepared to endorse the actual design plan as submitted. They judged that the alterations proposed would 'adversely affect the character ... of a protected structure of national importance'. That was a neat way of retaining control and presenting their heritage concerns as both predominant and determinative. The question now is whether any realistic modification towards meeting the requirements of liturgy will prove acceptable in a listed building where An Bord Pleanála can impose its veto. It was indeed a worrying development in what had come to be seen as a positive well-balanced partnership.

Perhaps some reorderings of churches in times past were done with little enough regard for heritage. That has cast a long shadow. In the case of St Colman's Cathedral the greatest care was taken to respect the architectural quality of the building in the proposed design plan for celebration of the liturgy. The original historic and beautiful sanctuary was not only preserved but was now in full view from the body of the church with the tabernacle still in its central location. The temporary wooden altar currently in place on the outer verge of the original sanctuary is not acceptable in terms of either liturgy or heritage. The question remains of finding a way forward from the current impasse. The best means of maintaining a historic church is to have it as a living House of God, a place for celebration of the liturgy with the active participation of the worshippers. Looking at the options will require not only further consultation with the heritage authorities but an approach to heal the breach with the parishioners in Cobh who have strenuously opposed the reordering.

The core group known as Friends of St Colman's Cathedral numbered among themselves people who held deep convictions that the cathedral sanctuary should remain essentially as it was. They were in agreement with the structural restorations but were not prepared to allow any realistic reordering. In their manifesto of 26 October 1999 it was stated: 'On behalf of the overwhelming majority of the people of the Great Island we are in favour of a replacement permanent wooden or marble altar *in the same location* as the present plywood altar.' In all honesty it is difficult to see how that proposed solution respects either the liturgical or the heritage requirements. One feels sure that this is open to further negotiation.

Those people of genuine conviction were poorly served by foot soldiers who were sent out on the campaigning trail to gather signatures throughout the diocese. I came into contact with some of them in Mallow. The message which they conveyed about likely alterations to the cathedral did not at all reflect what was actually being proposed. I would think that my experience was typical. If so the 40,000 or so signatures gathered throughout the diocese would have been very questionable.

As the process of reordering took its course, with the media cranking up the heat, more and more people up to then uninvolved became anxious that the emerging divisions in the community of Cobh could become chronic. This worry and concern spread through the diocese. In Cobh itself, particularly after the action of An Bord Pleanála, many ordinary people who had stood back from the campaign heretofore were now saying that enough was enough. Fostering further division in the community was seen as hurtful to everyone.

Up to then in parishes outside of Cobh there had been little interest in debating the pros and cons of the reordering. Very few attended the information meetings in the deaneries around the diocese. Now that accounts of the division in the community at Cobh began to percolate out the feeling began to grow generally that the cost to the community of driving the current project forward was becoming too high. This constituency of anxious people had begun to grow as we priests in the parishes came to appreciate.

Naturally I was personally very disappointed that the elegant and conservative design plan for reordering the sanctuary had failed to pass An Bord Pleanála. The wooden provisional altar, or any more permanent substitute installed on its current unsuitable site, would not be acceptable. As I write I hope and pray that good sense and good will may prevail to find a satisfactory solution. Perhaps in the intervention of An Bord Pleanála we may yet see a positive side in providing space for dialogue and healing of difference. One remembers how St Paul pleaded for unity in the church at Corinth: 'I do appeal to you, brothers, for the sake of our Lord Jesus Christ, to make up the differences between you, and instead of disagreeing among yourselves to be united in your belief and practice' (1 Corinthians 1:10). I feel that everyone should say Amen to that.

It is evident that of all of us Bishop John Magee was the one who most regretted the setback to a proper reordering of St Colman's Cathedral. He most of all knew what the proper celebration of the Church's liturgy required in terms of the clear understanding of that liturgy in the Second Vatican Council. In the Eastern Church the Sacred Mysteries were celebrated in the sanctuary which is divided by a screen or *iconostasis* from the nave where the congregation of lay faithful gathered. Even though St Colman's Cathedral did not incorporate an *iconostasis* the great distance of the high altar from the assembly of the faithful in the nave had something of the same effect. Would anyone today propose that we return to that pre-Vatican II system of celebration even with state-of-the-art lighting and amplification?

Everyone must appreciate that a proper reordering is required. The present provisional arrangement is not acceptable. It is not just a matter of replacing that wooden temporary altar. The location is simply not suitable. Would the replacing of the temporary altar become another moot point attracting the attention of An Bord Pleanála? On this they sit and await development. Their rationale of preserving heritage may not allow for any substantial alteration which seriously impacts on the existing sanctuary. What could be more substantial in a church than a proper siting of the altar of sacrifice? It is the focus of the liturgy and must be highlighted, not just added on as a practical measure. I feel certain that a satisfactory solution will be found through dialogue with those who share concern to have the cathedral serve as a living church for today's worshippers rather than be preserved as just a museum of heritage history. The challenge is to reconcile both concerns, heritage and liturgy. I am happy to end with the assessment of Fr Patrick Jones, Director of the National Centre for Liturgy in Maynooth:

> The sanctuary designed in the nineteenth century is certainly inadequate. Making some temporary adjustments in the 1960s is also inadequate. Leaving in place the historic elements but creating a larger space is often the solution. The creative spirit of artists and architects can contribute today to a building of another age. A contemporary sanctuary can be built in a historic building and, far from taking from its character, enriches it, as in the magnificent cathedral in the ancient German city of Trier, in Notre Dame in Paris and the Duomo in Milan. As well as this enrichment, it also keeps the building as a place of worship.
>
> (*The Irish Times*, 'Rite & Reason', 3 July 2006)

What has been achieved to date in restoring of the fabric of the cathedral is of outstanding quality. It will stand the test of time as the original did. It now stands to the credit of all those who made it possible. Bishop John Magee took the initiative in making the courageous decision to meet what was a major challenge. Canon Denis Reidy took on the responsibility of seeing the work through and has done so in superb fashion. The various committees which committed time, energy and expertise have shown the vast area of lay talents one can call on when work needs to be done. Then, of course, without a war chest the whole operation would be dead in the water. This is where the good-will of people right across the diocese made it all possible by the funds which they contributed.

It is unfortunate that the issue of the reordering of the sanctuary has proved so divisive. The media controversy has predominated to the effect that all the achievement to date no longer rates in public perception. It amounts to a major disappointment, particularly for Bishop John Magee and Canon Denis Reidy. However, the main concern now is to heal the divisions in the community. Time will allow for a calmer review of the options.

What will remain will be the memory of statistics piled up on the back of misleading information, intemperate language aimed at being personally offensive to our bishop and the fostering of divisiveness in the Christian community. In the process this discredited the campaign, whatever the rights and wrongs of the substantial issue. Those words of Jesus to the two Apostles, who were nicknamed Sons of Thunder, are relevant. They asked him to call down fire from heaven on a village which rejected them. 'Listen,' he said, 'do you not realise of what spirit you are?' Imagine the consequences of holding the requested public meeting to sort everything out! The bishop would have been happy enough to report back to the community on how matters were progressing but what a shambles a public meeting would turn out to be in the atmosphere then prevailing! For St Paul the touchstone to test the quality of any initiative or intervention was whether it would 'edify' the Christian community. Unfortunately that term has been weakened in our usage. For Paul it was the ultimate test. He would ask whether a particular course of action would positively help to build love and peace in the Christian community.

– THE BLIGHT OF CHILD SEX ABUSE –

The repeated charge of child sex abuse laid at the doors of institutions under religious control and of church personnel in various ministries has acted as a blight on Church morale and on the standing of the Church in the community. The trajectory of the charges reached back over forty years or more. The focus of those charges was not just the wrong behaviour of individual abusers but the inadequate manner in which Church authorities were seen to have dealt with the complaints.

In the moral textbooks with which I was familiar in Maynooth there would have been just a passing mention of paedophilia. It would have ranked in a lower case list with perversities such as bestiality and necrophilia. It merited little pastoral consideration because of the lack of appreciation of how common the practice was and of what serious damage it caused. The major concern would have been the scandal occasioned by the clerical perpetrators once their activities had become public.

This coloured how Church authorities dealt with complaints. Bishop or religious superior would have called in the alleged perpetrator and administered a serious warning. In blatant cases he would have referred the individual for psychiatric treatment. Typically he would transfer an accused to another area of ministry. This would be done more readily where specialist advice had assured that the risk of reoffending was now remote.

In early days there was little understanding even among professionals that paedophilia had such an obsessive compulsive factor which would strongly contraindicate any unsupervised access to children. Expressions of sincere repentance for the past and resolutions to avoid risks of reoffending in the future should not have been trusted in face of that strong tendency. It is accepted that where a transgression is opportunistic it should not qualify as out-and-out paedophilia, even though it would always have been a criminal offence. In public debate today the distinction is scarcely ever made.

In the event the manner in which Church authority dealt with the situation in times past is now described as a practice of 'cover-up' and proof of negligence in exposing other children to risk. These repeated charges have shattered public confidence in the institution and have brought the Catholic Church into disrepute, to the extent that it is no longer trusted to manage the situation. The Catholic Church has now been driven to accept that the matter should be almost exclusively managed by the civil authorities following codes of behaviour established by those authorities.

Sexual abuse of children is truly abhorrent. It is now well understood what long-term emotional damage it may cause to its innocent, vulnerable victims not only in their personal development but in their capacity later to form secure relationships. When a priest is at fault there is a serious breach of the trust where very often the family would have welcomed him into their home without any reservations. The priest abuser would have exploited the manner in which priests have been generally allowed unquestioned access to children. The resulting anger which affected the family because of the breach of trust and the damaging effect on the emotional and spiritual life of the child is quite understandable. The abuser would have been protected by the knowledge that the child would be unlikely to complain and that he or she would hardly be believed if they did same.

The scale of clerical sex abuse first emerged over twenty years ago in reports from the United States, Canada and Newfoundland. It was feared that the experience might be duplicated in Ireland. We were quickly brought to realise that it constituted a major problem here also. Incidents running from forty years ago were reported in the media. Complaints built up into considerable numbers. In 1996 the Catholic

Church compiled what came to be known as *The Framework Document* or the 'Green Book'. This set out a code of best practice for processing complaints in a context of pastoral care for all those affected. Nine years later an updated version *Our Children, Our Church* was introduced. In the meantime the *Report of the Ferns Enquiry* by Mr Justice Frank Murphy was published. This detailed account of the nature and extent of the clerical sex abuse of minors in one of Ireland's rural dioceses brought home the full impact of the issue. It gave credibility to the stringent procedures laid down in *Our Children, Our Church*. In these procedures the safety and well-being of children is paramount.

On confirming that there is at least a semblance of truth in an allegation and 'where reasonable grounds are established that child abuse has indeed occurred, the Director of Child Protection must report every allegation of abuse by a cleric, religious employee or volunteer of the Church to the civil authority immediately'. This commitment to report to the Gardaí has underlined the criminal nature of the offence and has operated as a further deterrent to any would-be offender. The likelihood of a Garda investigation has also proved a barrier to fraudulent claims. The 1998 Protection of Persons Reporting Child Abuse Act constitutes it a crime to make an allegation of child abuse that one knows to be false.

For a variety of reasons, chiefly with personal and family interests at stake, relatively few of those actually abused would be likely to come forward with complaints. The whole process with its inevitable publicity is traumatic. This circumstance surely affects conscientious people whose main concern would be that other children continue to be at risk. One expects that most abused people try to put it behind them and get on with their lives. Those who do come forward may have had a generally bad experience in life and then a counsellor will readily pick up on any abusive behaviour which they experienced in the past. It is accepted that most sexual abuse takes place with close relatives in the family circle or with neighbours. This leaves the priest an outsider who will very likely have moved on to another area. The repercussions of making a complaint will then be less than in the case of someone close to the victim. Still, we should not lose sight of the statistics that no more than 4 per cent of those charged are clerics.

In spite of the terrible experience suffered by Nora Wall, extensively reported in the media, one accepts that relatively few false complaints are lodged against accused who are still alive. They would inevitably do everything within their power to meet the charges and clear their names. The presumption that innocence until guilt is proved beyond reasonable doubt by the strict requirements of the criminal law is difficult to rebut. We know that priests and religious facing fraudulent claims go through hell on earth. There is simply no way that ultimate dismissal of the claim can restore the damage they suffer.

A questionable claim may be more likely to succeed where the alleged abuser is deceased. The accused is not there to marshall a defence. The outcome of a civil case for damages would then depend on the lesser standard of proof based on the balance of probabilities rather than the standard of 'beyond reasonable doubt' in the criminal trial. The action would of course also join the bishop where a claim for liability may be proved to attach to him as negligent in not forestalling the alleged abuse. The history of the Redress Board set up by the State to investigate abuse in residential centres does raise questions. The accused did not have proper opportunity to a defence against the charges, nor did the process allow for any real challenge. A minority of solicitors discovered a bonanza in the process.

One of the issues which has occasioned grief to priests is the requirement to step aside on administrative leave while the complaint is being processed. This requirement of stepping aside from ministry is presented as a precautionary measure, not as an indication of guilt. It applies in other professions as well, even though it is far more traumatic for the priest who does not have a private life or a home distinct from his place of work. In most situations the accused priest would in any case be under such severe stress that he would be unable to continue in his public ministry anyway. Nuala O'Loan, Police Ombudsman for Northern Ireland, has been critical of how some church authorities had implemented a requirement which had such serious implications for the priest: 'The Church should not by its actions create a situation in which priests are treated less fairly than others such as teachers, nurses, social workers and police officers' (*The Irish Times*, 14 March 2006). She takes particular exception to the practice of a bishop appearing in a church and making a formal announcement at an early stage in the enquiry.

In the Diocese of Cloyne Bishop Magee designated me as his delegate for processing complaints of clerical sex abuse. Even though we had the assistance of an outstanding case management committee with highly committed and well-qualified personnel I found the role stressful. Fortunately I had a lot of involvement in wider areas of ministry in parish and diocese as well as many other interests to occupy my mind. It would have been far more stressful if I had been occupied more or less full time with the demands of a role constantly bringing one face to face with the trauma of both complainant and accused. From the beginning we decided that our approach would be characterised as that of pastoral care for all those who were suffering the consequences of the sex abuse itself or the implications of the procedures put in place to deal with the complaint. After all, this pastoral care approach is where the Catholic Church finds itself at home in calling on long experience. Why should we put that experience aside and simply sign up to a list of civil procedures? Should not that pastoral care be the spirit in which we implemented those procedures? What emerged then as a result was a direct personal involvement with people rather than a cold professional client-based policy. As the experience of social workers in dealing with their clients teaches, this personal concern may indeed be fraught with risks of getting too involved oneself.

The model for any genuine Christian pastoral care is surely that mirrored in the Gospel parable of the Good Samaritan. The whole attitude and approach portrayed there is exemplary. I recall during my days in Maynooth working out with a group of satirically-minded students how today's hard-bitten professional world would address the situation confronting that Good Samaritan of the parable. The social strategist would have decided to establish a sub-committee to identify the causes of violence on the roads. The cautious legalist would have queried whether the mule was insured for third party transport, whether the casualty would suffer further injury through crude efforts to rescue him and whether the conditions in the hostel would measure up under the duty of care. The practical manager would have asked the Levite for the loan of his transport and would have begged money for the hostel from the priest.

That was all in light-hearted mood but then we came to analyse the attitudes and actions of the genuine Good Samaritan character in the parable. Without question his whole mindset and approach reflected the values which are at the very heart of the Gospel message. The compassion which he shows is inspired by unconditioned love for someone needing help here and now. He had not been accountable in any way for the current plight of the casualty. He is not concerned as to how far the casualty himself had contributed by his own carelessness through being in the wrong place at the wrong time. He acts with a spontaneous generous spirit. For him in the circumstances he can do no other but provide first aid as best he can in face of the presenting need.

That model of the Good Samaritan was relevant to our policy of pastoral care for all those affected by abusive behaviour. It went beyond satisfying oneself whether the diocese was or was not liable for the actions of the abuser. A professional lawyer might have advised that the diocese should not become involved in case that involvement could be interpreted in any way as an admission or an assumption of liability. Fortunately we were advised by an enlightened solicitor. Mr Diarmuid O'Catháin was of one mind with us on the matter of pastoral care. Indeed it was his idea from the beginning. He put any concerns in context by securing that assistance be provided on a good-will basis without prejudice. In the event, anyone suffering the consequences of sexual abuse would be treated with sensitivity and would be provided with professional help as needed. The call they made on our charitable resources was akin to that in a parish where a member of a family was in some trouble or other.

I have headed this section 'The Blight of Child Sex Abuse'. That is not an exaggeration. It has affected the morale of both bishops and priests: it has compromised the mutual trust between the bishop and his clergy; it has damaged the role of the Catholic Church as moral guide in the community; it has undermined the authority of that Church and its status as a valued institution in society; and it has constituted a waste of time and energy at a juncture which was crucial for implementing a general pastoral plan for the Church in Ireland as the contemporary world presented it with new challenges.

The moral climate in that world is now desperately in need of leadership. The reputation of almost every institution which has provided that world with solidity and solidarity has been subjected to public inquisition. Political, financial, legal, industrial and various other systems have been shaken out in a rolling process of iconoclasm. The Catholic Church in Ireland was traditionally at the centre of the community. It was a steadying influence because its place at that centre had general respect on its side.

I know that many priests blame the media for bringing the Church into disrepute. But what the media has exposed was already festering away beneath the surface. That rank infection had to be lanced sooner rather than later. Naturally enough, the media would have indulged a factor of *Schadenfreude* in doing that lancing. Many of those engaged in the media now found themselves on the high moral ground with the Catholic Church at the receiving end, that same Church which had exercised excessive control over them in the past. However, the media which had been busy dismantling the scaffolding which had supported society will now need in the interests of the common good to take a hand in the restoration.

Looking back we see how totally unprepared we were for the enormity of what came down the line. We are still facing some questions. Had our way of inculcating celibacy just as legal obligation exercised a negative influence on the clerical psyche? Is there something in the approach to sexuality in Irish culture which contributed to the problem? In this context the experience on the continent of Europe has been at a very moderate level in contrast to ours. This does leave us with a question.

Here in Ireland there is quite a difference between the negative reaction of people to the Church as institution and their positive feelings about their own priests. The evidence is that those feelings are as warm and supportive as ever, if not more so. That is my personal experience. People respect the priests in the parish and expect them to continue with their commitment as ever in the pastoral life. Sadly some priests lack the courage to proclaim what they are and so will no longer wear the clerical collar apart from in the exercise of their public ministry. I wear the collar without apology on public transport and on city streets. It has never attracted hostile glances nor adverse comments. If it did I would simply ignore them. I doubt that I would have come out on the spot with the riposte of one priest to an individual who had loudly proclaimed to all and sundry: 'They're all a pack of so-and-sos!' He took the wind out of the man's sails by advising that it is not proper in public to refer to one's family in those terms!

It is vital that the Catholic Church not lose courage after the ordeal it has been through in the past decade. Certainly the future exercise of its authority will take a new form. It has been refined in the crucible and much of that time-conditioned dross which has built up around it through an authoritarian mindset will have been burned off. It has been a humbling experience for all of us but that should promise well for the future, provided we read the signs of the times and adapt our approach to ministry. It would be unforgivable if in that ministry we should distance ourselves from children in the interest of self-protection as our predominant concern. In that case evil would have had its say through restricting us from positively presenting the message of the Gospel to children. All that would need is the negative body language which betrays an inner attitude of distrust. True enough, some priests uneasy in their ministry to children anyway will now cite a reason for distancing themselves even further. What then of the attitude of Jesus in warmly welcoming children into his company? Imagine what a positive effect that had on them.

Balance is everything, as the maxim has it. *Virtus in medio stat.* I vividly recall one incident, a straw in the wind which indicates that we may have gone too far in our concern with child protection. Has it become an obsession? Returning from a family outing to Innisfallen Island in Killarney one of the youngsters, a girl of seven or eight, fell into shallow water as I was mooring the boat. Straightaway I picked up the frightened child, hugged and reassured her as I brought her ashore. From a group on the pier a lady whom I knew said to me: 'Thank God, Father, you can still be yourself.' We have come to a sorry pass for this decent woman to feel called on to pass such a comment.

CHAPTER 6

LOOKING INTO THE FUTURE

Scanning back over the half century since my ordination to priesthood I am conscious above all else of a massive culture shift in Ireland. Much of that change is sourced from abroad, the result of greater exposure to dominant currents of opinion, chiefly in Europe and the United States. Continental Europe continues to be the major influence. Just look at how our legal, social and economic systems have been affected by various decisions of European courts and European commissions! We are no longer an island in any sense except that of geographic. More and more of our future direction is determined by outside forces.

Fifty years ago on 25 March 1947 the preamble to the Treaty of Rome was signed. On that momentous occasion the signatories committed themselves 'to establish the foundations for an ever closer union among the European peoples'. The German Chancellor Angela Merkel in her role as President of the EU now proclaims: 'We have to give a soul to Europe; we have to find Europe's soul.' When Ireland joined the EEC we had a vision that, just as the Irish missionaries had done in their golden age fifteen centuries ago, we would again invigorate the tired Europe. I well recall Dr William Philbin, then Bishop of Clonfert, setting out that vision in an inspiring booklet. When we moved to join the EEC little did we realise that it would be almost all one-way traffic as liberal secular values came to be the major influence on our legal, economic and social culture.

The world has shrunk around us. Our prosperity has now made it a ready option to travel from one side of the globe to the other – and travel far and wide we certainly do. I doubt if there is any country in the western world that equals Ireland in terms of fast forward in travel abroad – to take holidays, to visit friends, to do business, to reside in second homes. Then we have the increasing numbers of foreign people coming here to work and study. A generation back if you saw a black person on the street in Cork you would look again out of curiosity. That person would be judged a transient visitor. Now foreigners have settled here and come in increasing numbers from across the expanded European Union. The law forbids overt discrimination and harassment but rejection through attitude is more insidious. Inevitably there are racial tensions rumbling under the surface. These are far more widespread than what is said and done in public. That public reserve is motivated by legal sanction and political correctness.

The result is that through being so open to the world our culture is no longer self-contained as it was even a generation back. It will be a challenge from now on to preserve even remnants of our identity as a nation. That concern may not yet register with the generality of Irish people. One side effect of this exposure to outside influences and of this levelling of cultures will surely be that the conflict in Northern Ireland will gradually resolve itself on the ground. The black-and-white tribal lines of division will blur. As more and more young people from there study abroad and find work abroad they will see how fruitless and meaningless has been the situation at home.

I recall finding myself marooned late one night in the Murder Triangle around Caledon in South Armagh. I called to a well set-up farmer's house for directions. He went back to consult with the woman of the house. They both joined me at the door where the man said: 'We're God-fearing people and we cannot leave a fellow Christian in danger.' I was welcomed in. They were Presbyterians. They had never been south of the Border in their lives – just twenty miles away! We became good friends. James joined me on many a happy angling outing to Lough Sheelin. He often said that the Border ran through minds and hearts rather than through maps. May God rest him now in peace.

Our experience of unrivalled growth in material prosperity has established expectations of that high standard of living prevailing into the future. Current prosperity has certainly lifted the burden of hopeless impoverishment from many families. It has provided enhanced social services to the public and fuelled capital investment on infrastructure. We now see Irish people displaying entrepreneurial talents and business acumen quite unsuspected a generation ago.

Our experience of prosperity has been well charted by David McWilliams in *The Pope's Children*. One cannot disagree with his overview of how the flow of wealth has brought such radical changes in our way of life. He does it with a light touch but behind that is the analytic mind of a trained economist. The book has been well received by specialists in the field and has become a best seller for general readers. It does give a fair overview on where we have arrived in one generation. The questions now focus on the future.

In my schooldays it was common case in all the history and geography books of the time that Ireland was mainly – indeed almost exclusively! – an agricultural country. While there was heavy industry and value-added output in the north, we down here depended on export of our farm products. Ireland was said to be devoid of mineral wealth of any kind, if one discounted our bogs of which we had an abundance. We then appreciated the value of the contributions sent home by family members working abroad. They certainly helped our balance of payments.

– THE CRISIS IN CHURCH AUTHORITY –

That scan back over half a century is sufficient for our purposes here. It was within that earlier perspective a generation back that the Catholic Church came to exercise its central role in both community and society in Ireland. It really was a power in the land. Its authority was unquestioned. Bishops, priests and religious were treated with excessive respect and reverence. For what was later to come down the tracks that experience of life certainly did not qualify as adequate preparation for the priests of my time and even for those ordained twenty or thirty years later.

In terms of social attitude the biggest cultural change has been the erosion of authority. At the individual level the principle 'right to choose' has led people to take control of aspects of their lives where authority had formerly held sway. This change of attitude was facilitated by the many investigations into how institutions, which had been seen as bulwarks in society, had managed their affairs. Institutional authority lost credibility. That has applied right across the board on both religious and secular fronts. It affected the authority of the Catholic Church more than other sectors because its role in society and community at both religious and secular levels had been so directive and comprehensive. The writ of its jurisdiction by common consent had extended beyond the range of specific Church concerns into other areas where it was accorded or claimed an interest. It was not a healthy situation as time was to show. The Catholic Church felt the need to identify its role in society once the State had shaken itself free. This change of direction is quite evident in the approach taken by the bishops in their various pastoral letters which impinged on political interests. Some bishops quite openly welcomed this clear differentiation between the roles of Church and State.

The Catholic Church in Ireland had always been characterised by a level of religious practice unique in Europe. There it had been described rather dismissively as *Catholicisme du type Irlandais*. The perception there was that the Irish style of religion did not reflect personal faith conviction. That I have not accepted. The sense of Christian faith was woven into the Irish psyche. It expressed itself in day-to-day expressions which came as second nature to us. You will find a myriad of familiar examples in An t-Athair Diarmuid O'Laoghaire, *Ár bPaidreacha Dúthcais*. If our personal devotion and private prayer life did not reflect a genuine spirituality what else could? Perhaps a more questioning attitude would have helped towards a more mature faith.

If the Catholic faith were under direct attack, as happens in time of persecution, it would have been more treasured and more firmly rooted by that experience. This happened here under the Penal Laws and in Stalin's USSR. There the *babushka*, the grandmother, was a key figure in preserving the Christian faith over a generation of suppression. In Albania under the most uncompromising Stalinist regime of Enver Hoxha the Christian faith survived underground to blossom with extraordinary vigour given the opportunity. The Japanese martyrs Paul Miki and his twenty-five companions are still remembered in the liturgical calendar on their feastday, 6 February. They were crucified in Nagasaki in 1597 in the course of a persecution aimed at crushing the Christian religion. It is an amazing story of how afterwards a lay Christian community in Nagasaki survived underground without a priest for three hundred years!

The Catholic Church as institution in Ireland has been targeted across a broad front. Its credibility in every area has been questioned. Its sphere of influence has been curtailed. All the faults and exaggerations of power and influence in times past have been laid at its door. A suspicion of any kind which cast the Catholic Church in a bad light became grist to the media mill.

The credibility of individual bishops suffered as they were identified with the institution. Jesus spoke about how striking the shepherd leads to the dispersal of the flock. The more hostile attitude to the Catholic Church invaded the general culture which had traditionally been the matrix of Christian values as reflected in Catholic faith and practice. This shift in culture has led to an erosion of personal faith and a cold home for the practice of the Catholic religion. It also had its effect on the fall in vocations to the priesthood and religious life.

Catholic faith still finds a welcome refuge in current forms of community devotion. The growth of the Devotion to Divine Mercy has been phenomenal right across the land. This is no surprise. If Christians do not sense in their hearts the need for a Saviour and recognise in Jesus this same Saviour how can they call themselves Christian at all? Then in many parishes, as in Mallow, Perpetual Eucharistic Adoration has been established. This devotion is not an easy option. It has none of the shorter-term fervour that powers pilgrimages to Lourdes, Fatima and Medjugore. It has none of the expeditionary enthusiasm of climbing Croagh Patrick or visiting Lough Derg. These are certainly penitential exercises but they are of short duration. Committing oneself to pray an hour each week in the presence of the Blessed Sacrament is of quite a different character.

One is certainly inspired by those manifestations of genuine faith but one should not take too much comfort from them. The erosion of respect for the authority of the Catholic Church across an increasing spectrum of Irish life is self-evident. Here we may speak of a crisis in religion, if we take religion as allegiance to a body of doctrine and system of practice. We see the decline reflected in permissive behaviour where self-indulgence rules under the banners of the ancient idols of Mammon, Venus and Bacchus. Indeed there is a sense of self-righteousness particularly among media people in turning one's back on Catholic tradition.

– COURAGE TO DECLARE ONESELF A CATHOLIC –

One is struck by how many people, many of whom are leaders of public opinion, openly take some pride in admitting that they are no longer Catholic. A Church of England friend perceives a radical difference in media attitudes to religion between Ireland and Britain. It takes courage now for a lay person, particularly one in the public eye, to declare oneself a Catholic or to be perceived as a Catholic. When Professor Patricia Casey engaged with the Iona Institute her objectivity and credibility as a professional psychiatrist were questioned because of that close association with a professedly religious body connected to the Catholic Church. This singling out of one's religious conviction as a bar to objectivity and credibility betrays prejudice. Imagine the outcry if an environmentalist were to suffer criticism because he or she was appointed to the National Roads Authority! Is it now accepted wisdom that objectivity is confined to representatives of a favoured viewpoint?

Two columnists in *The Irish Times*, Breda O'Brien and William Reville, stand out in exercising their 'right to choose' when they declare openly that they are Catholic. It represents a challenge to those who claim the high moral ground of political correctness. In a critical comment on *The God Delusion* by Richard Dawkins, William Reville asked: 'Why doesn't he take on the new secular religion of political correctness (PC) which has silently taken over public life in recent decades? PC is anti-scientific, makes people afraid to think certain thoughts, closes down whole areas of debate, publicly vilifies people who diverge from accepted beliefs, and is rife on university campuses.' (*The Irish Times*, 4 January 2007)

We accept that in Ireland there is a crisis in religion. Where religion might have been once regarded in principle as an anchor for good order it has drifted with the current of the culture shift. Is there also a crisis in personal conviction in which any genuine religion should have its roots? This is a more serious question. What do people mean when they say that they are not religious while they claim to have a sense of the spiritual? For many this signifies that they feel a need for God as a caring presence in their lives. How often we hear someone say that even though they do not practise any religion they do pray in the face of some problem or other? They say that while they may have lost faith in the Catholic Church they have not lost faith in Jesus.

Many others distance themselves from a personal God. They feel a deep need to experience something of what John O'Donoghue reads into Celtic spirituality in his many books. They will have a particular affinity with the concept of a divine presence in nature such as that described in the ancient Celtic poem of Amergin:

> I am the wind that breathes upon the sea,
> I am the wave of the ocean,
> I am the murmur of the billows,
> I am the ox of the seven combats,
> I am the vulture upon the rock,
> I am a beam of the sun,
> I am a wild boar in valour,
> I am a salmon in the water,
> I am a lake in the plain,
> I am a word of science,
> I am the point of the lance of battle,
> I am the God who creates in the head the fire.
>
> Who is it who throws light into the meeting on the mountain?
> Who announces the ages of the moon (If not I)?
> Who teaches the place where couches the sun (If not I)?

I feel that very few declare themselves out-and-out atheists. Most would stay with the more logical description of agnostics. Of course quite a large number of people are practical atheists. They have simply dismissed any thought of God from their lives as inconvenient or irrelevant. One is reminded of the cartoon which portrays a roguish character with a woman on one arm and a six-pack under the other. The legend reads, 'Thank God, I am an atheist!'

It all adds to the feeling that we are swept along in the dust trail of the Celtic Tiger. We are intoxicated with our current prosperity and with the confidence which it instils that there is more of the same ahead. It is a heady atmosphere. Prophets of doom will not get a hearing. Look at how we ignore the mountain of debt piling up on individuals and families through heavy mortgages and financing lifestyles through credit? As Troy was facing destruction the warnings of the prophetess Cassandra were ignored.

We currently have a young generation which has not had to cope with hardship or with any downturn on their life expectations. In fact our culture aims to build up self-esteem and assure the young that they can and should be high achievers. Whatever self-belief they have, life is a tough taskmaster. It inevitably prunes back unrealistic self-confidence. Currently educational psychologists in the Untied States are stressing the need for a saner balance. Inflated expectations of life may later prove lethal and then addiction to drugs and recourse to suicide may be seen to offer escape routes from reality. Traditionally in our Christian faith and allegiance to religious practice we had a sure compass through the shifting sands and ups-and-downs of life. One hopes that the influences which would relegate faith to the margins of consciousness and which have compromised commitment to religious belief and practice have not penetrated to the roots. The radical secularisation of French culture took centuries rather than decades to predominate. Ireland is now also *pays de mission*. A single generation of questioning here in Ireland will not have uprooted the faith of centuries, provided we as the Church grasp the current challenge as opportunity into the future.

– PUTTING OUT INTO THE DEEP –

Nostalgia for the past and pulling the wagons into a circle in the vain hope that the crisis will pass is a counsel for failure.

The challenge is to identify whither the Spirit is leading and directing into the future. As Pope John XXIII said on launching of the Second Vatican Council, we must identify the signs of the times. This will be a painful experience as we leave the familiar shore and launch out into the deep. John the Baptist summing up his role in relation to Jesus said: 'He must increase, I must decrease.'

Traditionally we had solid structures in place which served us well in establishing the concept of Church for its time. The clergy took the leading role in every area. Charisms and particular callings which did not fall in with our expectations of what the Catholic Church in Ireland was about or should be about tended to wither on the vine. Other countries, even those in which Irish missionaries worked, might go their own ways, but in Ireland we had a system of 'one size fits all'. I have already said that in Ireland we failed to draw on the experience of our missionaries and on those Irish priests who had been chosen to head up international orders. One is reminded of the mythical Procrustes and that bed of his.

The ideal requirement of anyone entrusted with authority in our Church was to have a safe pair of hands. Prudence, understood in the negative sense of holding the line, was the basic requisite. All too readily prudence would have become the cuckoo in the nest which tended to push other pastoral virtues out to the side, particularly where new initiatives were involved. In the teaching of St Thomas Aquinas prudence was defined positively as choice of the most effective means towards achieving desired spiritual and pastoral goals.

I have already spoken of the high academic standard typical of the student cohorts in the Maynooth of my time. In addition to that academic promise they had entered on the priesthood as all-rounders in terms of their human qualities. They would have been high achievers in any profession, in any walk of life or in any branch of business. They related well to one another in a general atmosphere of give-and-take and good humour. Discipline in observing college rules was certainly required but it never snuffed out our humanity. Those few who came to recognise, or were brought to recognise, that they did not have a vocation for priesthood went, as the Latin tag described it, *ad vota secularia*. In that lay world they almost invariably made their mark as leaders and high achievers in their chosen professions.

Now for the crucial question! Why did their contemporaries in the diocesan priesthood not produce more leaders and high achievers in pushing ahead with pastoral initiatives? Certainly there are people who have pushed out into the deep like my classmate Monsignor Denis Faul in Northern Ireland and Fr Harry Bohan of the Céifin Institute in Ennis. But how many more of us were well enough satisfied to follow along the well trodden track beaten out by the generations ahead of us. That was all that was expected of us. These thoughts strongly lodged with me when I recently attended the funeral Mass of Canon Bertie Troy, late Parish Priest of Midleton, a close contemporary of mine. He was much loved in all the parishes in which he had ministered. In that parish context he was everything a pastor should be. It was in Bishop Magee's homily at the Mass and in the GAA County Secretary's address at the graveside that another side to Canon Bertie was highlighted: his outstanding leadership in coaching Cork hurling teams to eleven All-Ireland victories. What a record in a very competitive national sport! Everyone remarked on his talents for planning strategies and for inspiring teams to give of their best.

I could name others such as the late Dean John Thornhill of Youghal, an outstanding pastor of the old school. He too had leadership promise as reflected in the high regard in which he was held by his brother priests. Imagine if that quality had been released into positively identifying pastoral initiatives! It was said of him at his funeral that his programme of life had not altered since his student days in Maynooth. Evidently the system with which we had identified ourselves did not challenge us to read what Pope John XXIII had referred to on the eve of Vatican II as 'the signs of the times'.

I was in Rome as that Council was due to begin. I have spoken already about how it quickly became evident that Ireland was in a backwater. We were not in a good position to offer leadership to the bishops of our diaspora. That would have been understandable if the Council were set to follow down the line of the First Vatican Council with its emphasis on more theological and doctrinal matters. We would not have been up to speed on academic theology as in Continental university settings. But Vatican II was proclaimed as a Pastoral Council! We in Ireland had always prized our reputation as a Church which had a strong and well proven pastoral orientation. It quickly emerged that we were not in a position to help in answering questions which we had not yet seriously addressed for ourselves.

We who were on the theological staff in Maynooth have our own critical questions to address. We may say that after the Council we were too engaged with structures within the College to commit as much concern as we should have done to the trajectory of that Council. However, the crucial time was the decade or so before the Council took place. Did we read the signs of the times? I have already said that the one person on our staff who did so was Canon JG McGarry, founding father and editor of *The Furrow*. He chose the title from the Vulgate Latin text of the prophet Jeremiah 4:3: *Novate vobis novale* (yours to plough a new furrow). How apt a title it was for the pastoral concerns which were addressed by those whom he invited to contribute to its pages! Looking back over half a century *The Furrow* appeared like the Morning Star lighting the dawn of a new day. At the time we did not read to where that sign beckoned. Neither did we appreciate the maelstrom of white water which awaited us outside the lagoon. The crisis was ahead. Would we welcome it as kairos or crisis?

Jesus said: 'The children of this world are wiser in their generation than the children of light.' We have seen how Irish entrepreneurs have emerged on all sides to respond to the opportunities offered by the European Union and the interlinking of the world economy. They have read the signs of the times, measured up to the challenges and planned their strategies accordingly. We can read it all in the spoor of the so-called Celtic Tiger. It may be brash and merciless but it reads as success in their terms. It certainly leaves us with questions to answer in terms of our progress in responding to pastoral challenges in the mission of making Christ present in this new world. The Irish entrepreneurs who have forged ahead in their world are no different in nature from us in Church ministry.

– PASTORAL STRATEGY INTO THE FUTURE –

At the turn of this century the late John Paul II stressed to the Irish bishops on their *Ad limina* visit to Rome the pressing need for a diocesan pastoral plan. A pastoral plan requires that we identify the longer term needs and challenges, that we assess opportunities and resources, that we put into action the necessary strategies to meet those needs and challenges. Above all it must be a solidly practical rather than an abstract vision. We certainly do need vision to read those challenges as opportunities.

One challenge which is currently confronting all of us is the increasing shortage of priests to minister to the Christian community into the future. In Mallow itself we had drawn up plans to divide the parish northside and southside with the Blackwater as common boundary. It made good sense some years back as the population was already increasing around a town which had been identified as a 'hub' in the overall spatial strategy for fast forward development. We already had the structures in place for the planned division when it was brought home to us that the number of priests in the diocese into the future would call more for clustering of parish ministry rather than division. The current model in the Diocese of Killaloe would soon be universal as fewer priests will be in ministry.

We know that centuries back the Catholic Church ministered with fewer priests in pastoral work in Ireland. We recall how in the 1940s and 1950s seminaries then expanded in response to the flood of vocations to priesthood. However that was in a very different religious culture. The decline in numbers over recent years has accelerated with the older cohort of priests now at retiring age, many younger priests leaving the ministry, and far fewer entering seminaries. We certainly hope and pray that the decline will be corrected and that today's sense of challenge will inspire the high minded and high spirited to answer the call of Jesus: 'Come, follow me'.

For now we must take account of the situation as it is. Killaloe has taken early steps on the way by introducing lay people into administrative and management roles as back-up to the clustering of parishes. This will soon become the universal pattern. The practice of priests counting and banking parish funds, chairing school boards of management and monitoring every detail in the administration of a parish will soon be consigned to history. It is a matter of determining priorities. Through sharing out these administrative roles, in which people in the world of work and business should be particularly qualified, priests are released for their specific sacramental and pastoral roles.

We see how effective pastoral councils and finance councils can be in the running of a parish. This recognition of the management talents of lay people is surely welcome. One regrets that the urgency now comes as a response to a crisis situation rather than as a matter of principle. I have spoken already of the good advice given by Niall Crowley, chairman of Allied Irish Banks, who had personally engaged time and talent in the planning of the John Paul II Library in Maynooth. Having discovered that Mallow did not have a parish centre he was adamant with his laconic comment: 'Buy it or build it.' What superb advice that was! As the years roll on the parish centre in Mallow is seen by priests and people as an absolute treasure. Both of the secretaries, Martina Aherne and Anne

Scully, have been able to manage the day-to-day work of parish administration. Total loyalty and family team spirit mark that service to the parish. Every large parish needs a parish office and a secretary not only to release priests for their more specific pastoral roles and provide the resources to exercise those roles more effectively, but to provide people with the services they require and expect. There may not even be a proper filing system, which leaves a parish rudderless, particularly when there is a change of personnel in the priest team. Currently Mallow has three second-level schools and six primary schools. Each employs a secretary. That surely makes the case for a parish office. In smaller parishes a few hours per week of professional service make such a difference in the assistance offered to priest and people.

On the more spiritual side of lay ministry we have lay people participating in the Liturgy as Readers of the Word or as Ministers of the Eucharist. Beyond that we have many lay people collaborating with teachers in preparation for the Sacraments and in other pastoral roles in parish and dioceses. Our teachers exercise the role of catechist and are truly lay ministers of Word and Eucharist akin to catechists in missionary territories. In the teaching of the Church the concept of lay ministry hinges on the significance of a call through Baptism and Confirmation addressed to all Christians. The words of Jesus 'Go out to the whole world and preach the Gospel' were certainly addressed to the Apostles, but they were not confined to them. Currently the Catholic Church here is preparing to introduce the diaconate. This is timely and welcome. This measure of ordained ministry will not render the call to lay ministry redundant. Up to now we have been speaking about lay people volunteering their talents and skills to assist in Church administration and ministry. An important area on which we need to concentrate minds will be on that of employing qualified committed lay people to serve in full-time ministry. Many people with that vocation have acquired degrees up to postgraduate level in doctrinal and pastoral theology through Maynooth, Mater Dei and similar institutions. Integrating those with that special charism for ministry will prove sensitive, even though it is inspired by the Holy Spirit who, like the wind, blows when and where he wills.

Where lay ministry is hived off in a very specific role, such as chaplaincy in a school, this is generally acceptable. It is when someone is appointed to a key role as part of a ministry team in parish or diocese that collaboration or partnership may prove uneasy. This is where clericalism comes into the picture – and the virus of clericalism is not confined to clergy, but it is contagious. Questions about the expense to diocese or parish will surface early, even when there is hardly ever question about what is expended in building and restoring churches and in other bricks-and-mortar structures.

Behind this criticism about cost there is more likely than not a concern about the nature of ministry which a qualified and committed lay person may now provide. Justice does require that we pay a person of that quality and expertise at least the equivalent of a teacher's salary in one of our schools. The tensions arise when a lay pastoral minister with a proactive vision impinges on our comfort zone, be it personal or pastoral. Maybe we discover that instead of the workhorse we anticipated we now find ourselves landed with a thoroughbred! These are challenging times which demand new vision, fresh initiatives and new management skills. When we see how full-time lay ministers have been integrated into diocesan and parish teams in other lands our current reservations will become history. Let it be a nail in the coffin of clericalism. I trust that I will be around to celebrate the funeral.

Personally I have had the good fortune to experience pastoral life in some model parishes, particularly in Australia and New Zealand. A generation ago the Church culture there mirrored that of Ireland. There has been a radical restructuring meanwhile. Sociologists analyse the interplay between attitudes and systems. Imposing a new system before attitudes are ready to accept it will prove counterproductive. It is the parable of the new patch stitched into the old garment. Attitudes are best transformed by personal experience through seeing a system at work in similar circumstances elsewhere. Now with the reasonable cost of travel we Irish priests have the opportunity of observing collaborative ministry at work in other places.

Without question the pastoral culture of the Catholic Church in Ireland will experience a sea change before the century is much older. Currently the old maxim *Festina lente* recommends that haste be made at a gentle pace, the speed of the slowest camel. We do respect the cautionary note in that parable of Jesus that pouring new fermenting wine into old cracked skin bottles will burst the bottles and lose the wine. We have urgent work to do in replacing those old bottles. There is no time like the present. The Psalmist said, 'Today if you hear his voice harden not your hearts'.

– THE ROAD AHEAD –

As title for this memoir I chose words from that challenge of Jesus to those who would follow him: 'No one putting hand to the plough and looking back is fit for the Kingdom of Heaven.' When I personally put hand to the plough there was no single blinding moment of truth like that of Paul on the road to Damascus. I suppose there was that solemn moment at Ordination when one made the formal response to undertake and fulfil the duties of a priest: 'Yes, with the help of God.'

However, that response was long in preparation through a conditioning process. The seed was planted through a wholesome family life in Meelin and confirmed by the ethos of that supportive community. As models I had those wonderful priests of whom I have spoken. Finally in St Colman's College and in Maynooth the compass was set and the helm locked on a course of 'steady as she goes'. When Archbishop McQuaid asked whether I was ready to respond to the challenges of priestly ministry I was firm in my response: 'Yes, with the help of God.'

I thank God that I have never regretted that yes. If I had a life to spend over again I sure would change those areas where I could have done better as man and priest but the overall direction would not alter. The motivation would have deepened. To continue the metaphor of Jesus I have not looked back from the plough. I have been blessed with such friends over the last fifty years. They have kept my feet solidly on the ground and confirmed me in my vocation as priest. I find that women who are really at ease with you are more honest and forthcoming when it comes to communicating 'home truths'. A man prevaricates in case he offends. A woman finds words, as St Paul said, to speak the truth in love.

Given the human condition, I count myself as having had a really contented and fulfilled life over those seventy-five years. There were sad, dark times at intervals. Fortunately I am fairly stoical and always had the sensitive support of friends. From experience I learned the difference between empathy and sympathy. In empathy one communicates at a deep, sensitive level and so less is said in words. In the phrase of the Psalmist, *Cor ad cor loquitur:* heart speaks to heart. Sympathy can all too easily be cloying and superficial. It may strike a false note, a note of self-indulgence.

I recall a singular example of that. I knew someone who would be described as 'living for wakes and funerals'. When asked whether she was coming to the wake she might well reply: 'Yes, I am – who's dead?' On arrival she would take up her keening note even though, as so often in rural Ireland, the wake had now moved on to another phase. I attended one such wake when our friend arrived late and launched into her usual lament. The lament silenced the talk of the company around the big open fire. The son of the deceased rose to his feet, placed his hands on the door posts of the corpse room and pronounced: 'For God's sake, won't you join us for a cup of tea and don't carry on there indulging yourself!'

From my Maynooth days I recall Aristotle's analysis of happiness. His basic principle was 'Everyone desires happiness'. They may take various roads in pursuit of that human happiness but sooner or later the false trails will run into the sand. Happiness for Aristotle was self-fulfilment. The possession of material things or the experience of pleasure would not qualify. In fact, the maxim of Socrates would be true that one finds happiness in proportion to what one can do without. Diogenes of Syracuse in that tub of his had been so content with his choice of lifestyle that his only request to Alexander the Great was that the conqueror of all the earth should stand to one side as he was blocking the sunlight. In following a vocation inspired by Christian love and pastoral care we have the ideal avenue to personal happiness as well.

One of the best analyses of clergy morale in the Irish scene which has come my way is that short article by Fr Aidan Ryan in *The Furrow* of December 2006. He ministers as a priest in Ballinahown, Co. Westmeath. He has put a great deal of thought into a well balanced, down-to-earth assessment of how we priests should cope with stress and ward off any drop in morale. It has the quality of personal witness. Having listed the positive factors in one's life as a priest which make for all-round well-being he comes to the heart of the matter. Here I quote the text:

> Only faith gives sense and meaning to how we live our lives, and faith of the depth needed for the wholesome and happy living of the priesthood can be sustained only by a strong and committed prayer life. Prayer on its own, of course, will not ensure a good personal morale unless it is supported by some combination of the other elements mentioned previously. Grace must build on nature, but without faith sustained by prayer, it is difficult to see how the priesthood makes any kind of sense. And if a life does not make sense, it

is very difficult to see how it can be lived with that combination of commitment, enthusiasm, contentment and fulfilment which we indicate when we use the word 'morale'.

All I can add is a simple comment 'That's the spirit!' One of the positive elements in life which he lists is a sense of humour: 'The capacity for not taking ourselves or life around us too terribly seriously is a great blessing.' Let Jesus have the last word in reminding us to trust in God the Father's loving care: 'Can any of you, for all his worrying, add one single cubit to his span of life? ... So do not worry about tomorrow: tomorrow will take care of itself. Each day has enough trouble of its own' (Matthew 25–34).

Speaking about morale we must question whether we priests are helping ourselves as much as we used to do, and as much as we should now do. In my early days as priest I recall happy, indeed uproarious sessions with characters such as Fr Phil Mortell. As I am writing this the races at Cheltenham are in full swing. That had been one of his stamping grounds. From there he would radiate to London and then home, having taken 'the waters' at Bath. Back at base he would host a dinner at which he would regale the company with his experiences which, like himself, would be larger than life. He actually did weigh twenty-two stone in the whole of his health! That provided material for his encounter with an electronic weighing scales in London. He claimed that it came to pass in a gaming arcade where he had taken shelter from a hail storm. On stepping on the scales he was greeted by a shrill voice from the machine: 'One at a time, please!'

Phil Mortell, God rest him, was unique but there were many others in that same company. As a young man my role was to listen respectfully to my elders. My total recall of so many incidents proves that there was a lot to listen to in those exchanges. The one time when I would be consulted would be when some issue of theology was introduced. This would not be unusual. Phil Mortell would have primed himself well. He was widely read with a sharp intellect behind the easy camaraderie. That pen portrait of Phil gives a flavour of the clerical culture of the mid-1950s. Phil would celebrate that culture in the verse which he attributed to Hilaire Belloc:

> Wher'ere a Catholic sun doth shine
> There's always laughter and good red wine.
> At least I have always found it so.
> Benedicamus Domino.

Today we live in a quite different culture. Very many priests spin out quite lonely lives. All too often their houses are not homes. The live-in priest's housekeeper is now unusual. In former times even having someone to answer the telephone kept a light in the house. The dinner in the priest's house celebrating Christmas was an occasion for a get-together. Now priests across the generations may hardly know one another. Some groups do meet for prayer and *Lectio Divina* and prepare scriptural homilies together. In general we see one another only at funerals and at formal meetings of official diocesan committees. One pundit tired of meetings composed the prayer: 'Forgive us our conferences as we forgive those who conference against us.' We are isolated from one another more than we need be by travelling alone rather than with others on our way to such meetings. Admittedly there may be other appointments to be met in the offing. We will need real fraternity for the challenge ahead.

I believe that there are core values at risk in our culture and that a radical prophetic programme of pastoral action is called for if we are to meet the challenge. That challenge will be an opportunity to present the Gospel to people as making sense of life for themselves and for their children. As I write the controversy continues about Taoiseach Bertie Ahern's reference to 'aggressive secularism' as on the march in Irish culture today. As people come to realise the moral vacuum to which aggressive secularism leads, we Christians, who are entrusted with Christ's mandate to preach the Gospel, will join with all others of similar mind to let the light shine in the darkness that would otherwise engulf us. At a recent Céifin conference in Ennis, Ombudsman Emily O'Reilly made reference to people considering their position and tip-toeing back to the churches. We may not have long to wait, but we must be ready with good answers to the concerns which will present.

On the occasion of his pastoral visit to the World Congress of Families at Valencia in Spain in July 2006 Pope Benedict was asked by a German journalist why he had omitted the expected denunciations of such issues as gay unions and gay adoptions. His response was enlightening. 'Christianity, Catholicism, is not a collection of prohibitions; it is a positive option. It is very important that we look at this matter again, because this idea has almost completely disappeared today. We have heard so much about what is not allowed that it is now time to say that we have a positive message to offer.'

Currently we in Ireland are ensnared in a net of specific moral and social issues which determine the agenda for the Church. These issues have become the principal preoccupations of the public forum so that it proves well nigh impossible for the Church to establish a positive balance in pastoral ministry. This is certainly what Pope Benedict had in mind in his comments at Valencia.

In the Vatican Council's Declaration on Religious Freedom we find inspiration for pastoral ministry in today's world: 'The truth cannot impose itself except by virtue of its own truth as it makes its entry into the mind at once quietly and with power.' It takes a prophet to discern that truth and then address it convincingly to the searching mind. The Spirit of Truth who guides the transmission of the Gospel message will inspire the response of that searching mind.

AFTERGLOW

As I was drawing this memoir to a close I came to walk with the red setters Deise and Cora along the quiet road in Ballintona which was once my home stamping ground. I leaned over the Black Bridge under which the Dallow meanders its way to join the Blackwater. Memory rolls back the years to those happy days when my angling friends and I would discuss the weather and the fishing conditions. Then as now things were never as good as they used to be!

It seems only yesterday when 'fond memory brings the light of other days around me'. A lot of water has passed under that bridge in the meantime. Two-thousand-five-hundred years ago the Greek philosopher Heraclitus said that one cannot stand in the same river twice. Still as I looked around everything seemed familiar enough with a bittersweet quality. When Patrick Kavanagh paid a visit back to his homestead in Monaghan he put his feelings in verse. Let those thoughts of his stand for me as well.

> A tree, a stone or a field
> Recreates for us the happiest –
> And the saddest –
> Which is the same thing –
> In other words our moments
> Of most intense experience.

One of the blessings of life into one's seventies is happy memories – or is it to be able to focus on those rather than on the regrets! I thank God for a life which found such interest in human nature with all its foibles. When in Maynooth we studied in classical literature the Roman dramatist Terence. He summed up his experience of life in similar words. *Homo sum, humani nil a me alienum puto.* When all is said and done what is Christian living but the human writ large in the light of the Gospel!